LITTERA ET SENSUS

LITTERA ET SENSUS

Essays on Form and Meaning in Medieval French Literature presented to John Fox

edited by D.A. Trotter

UNIVERSITY OF EXETER

First published 1989 by the
University of Exeter
Copyright © 1989 D.A. Trotter and
the several authors each in respect of the paper contributed.
ISBN   0   85989   333   2

University of Exeter
Publications Office
Reed Hall
Streatham Drive
Exeter EX4 4QR

Set in 10 on 12, 9 on 10 and 8 on 9 pt Garamond

Printed in Great Britain at the Alden Press
Oxford London and Northampton

CONTENTS

Preface

This volume contains the papers given at the Colloquium in Honour of Professor John Fox held at the University of Exeter in September, 1988. One paper has been omitted, since the findings embodied in it are shortly to be published elsewhere. Avril Henry's paper, given on the first evening, consisted of an illustrated presentation of the Eton Roundels. In these richly-ornamented *figurae Bibliorum*, an elaborate and theologically complex message is unfolded both in the detailed construction of each element, and, above all, through the relationship between constituent parts and the general disposition of the whole. Form and meaning become synonymous: *signifiant* and *signifié* coalesce to provide what is, literally, a revelation.[1]

Such contemplation of the sacred provided a fitting prelude to this colloquium on Form and Meaning, and to the more secular contributions of the other speakers. These have been printed below in the order in which they were delivered. I should like to take this opportunity to express my gratitude to Mrs Barbara Mennell, of the Publications Office of the University of Exeter, for the care and expertise which she devoted to the production of this volume.

D.A. Trotter
Exeter, July 1989

---

1 Dr Henry's findings are to be published as *The Eton Roundels: Eton MS 177 'Figurae Bibliorum'* (Aldershot, Scolar-Gower, 1989).

John Fox

People retire to Devon . . . Yet such a thought was far from the mind of John Howard Fox when, as a young (by modern standards, very young) Assistant Lecturer, he took up his post in the Department of French at the University College of the South West in 1948. Yet this Yorkshireman, graduate of University College, Hull, with a Yorkshireman's sense of humour and witty raconteur style, was to make Exeter his home for the rest of his career. Hundreds, indeed thousands, of undergraduates will remember his resounding tones as he explained and illustrated the evolution of the French language from Claassical Latin to the present day. His inimitable way of casting light upon the arcane mysteries of medieval literature opened the eyes of many to its inherent beauty and wisdom; many were so inspired that they continued their interest into research and are now in university posts up and down the country.

From his first appointment, he moved through the grades of Lecturer (1950) and Reader (1964) to be elected to a Chair of French in 1967. He has been Head of the Department of French and Italian (1975–82) and Dean of the Faculty of Arts (1979–82). The University has changed much in the last forty years and John Fox has played an important role in the transformation of the former University College of the South West into the present firmly-established University of Exeter. Through his sustained endeavour the status of French Studies has been greatly enhanced. His contribution to life at the University of Exeter and to the propagation of French culture both nationally and internationally was recognised by the French Government in 1983 when he was created *Chevalier dans l'ordre des Palmes académiques*, for *services rendus à la culture française*.

It is chiefly with medieval studies that John Fox's name is associated and for many years he has represented them on the Editorial Board of *French Studies*. His own publications are wide-ranging, his first book being on *Robert de Blois, son œuvre didactique et narrative*; subsequently, he was drawn more and more towards the poetry of the Middle Ages, especially that of François Villon, an attraction which still goes on, and to the lyric poetry of Charles d'Orléans, leading to a book which he had the satisfaction and honour of seeing translated into French. He is in no way, however, a narrow specialist and the extent of his scholarship can be gauged from the volume he devoted to the Middle Ages in the *Literary History of France*, which encompasses the earliest extant texts of the ninth century and the *chansons de geste*, the lives of the saints and the *Roman de la Rose*. Students who have sweated over the vagaries of the emergence of French from Vulgar Latin are indebted to him for his short, but valuable book written in collaboration with Robin Wood, *A Concise History of the French Language (Phonology and Morphology)*.

A lover, strange as it may seem, of fast vehicles and outdoor activites, John Fox is very much a 'doing' man. He has great personal energy and dynamism. For many years the Foxes — John and his first wife Jacqueline — were familar figures on the campus, as they took their morning walk, always engrossed in what seemed like intense conversation, to Queen's Building. When Jacqueline died in 1984, her death was a tragic loss not only to John and his family but also to the Department.

Although not attracted temperamentally by the administrative side of academic life, John has performed his duties with the same meticulous attention to detail and the same desire to maintain standards that have been characteristic of both his research and his teaching.

Those of us who have been privileged to work with him, be taught by him, to have researched with him or simply just to have known him, extend to him in the form of this collection of essays our warmest thanks for all he has achieved and our best wishes to him and Riki, his second wife, for what promises to be an active, continuing career.

Robert Niklaus

Keith Cameron

A Bibliography of John Fox's Writings

Books

Robert de Blois, son oeuvre didactique et narrative (Librarie Nizet, Paris (V^e), 1950, 194 pp.).

The Poetry of Villon (Thomas Nelson, London, 1962, xxiii + 169 pp.). Reprinted in 1976 by Greenwood Press, Connecticut.

Introduction, bibliography and explanatory notes to *Complete Poems of François Villon*, translated by Beram Saklatvala (Dent, London, 1968), pp. xxv, 185–201.

The Lyric Poetry of Charles d'Orléans (Clarendon Press, Oxford, 1969, xiv + 163 pp.). Translated into French as *La Poésie Lyrique de Charles d'Orléans* (Nizet, Paris, 1971).

Charles d'Orleans, *Choix de Poésies*, Editées d'après le ms Royal 16 F II du British Museum par John Fox, *Textes littéraires*, Vol. IX (University of Exeter, 1973, xxxi + 54 pp.).

'The Middle Ages', Vol I, in *A Literary History of France* (Ernest Benn Limited, London, 1974, 380 pp.).

'The Charlemagne Legends', 'The Medieval Troy Legends', 'Alexander the Great — in Western Europe', in *Legends of the World*, ed. Richard Cavendish, (Orbis, London, 1982), pp. 216–234.

Villon: Poems, Critical Guides to French Texts (Grant & Cutler, London, 1984, 108 pp.).

Fifteenth-Century French Poetry (Grant & Cutler, London) (forthcoming).

An Anthology of Fifteenth-Century French Poetry (Grant & Cutler, London) (forthcoming).

Articles

'The Date and Composition of Villon's *Testament*', *French Studies*, 7 (1953), 310–22.

'Two Borrowed Expressions in the "Charroi de Nîmes"', *Modern Language Review*, 50 (1955), 315–17.

'L'Affaiblissement de R devant Consonne dans la Syllabe Protonique en Moyen Français', *Revue de Linguistique Romane*, 22 (1958), 92–7.

'A Note on Villon's "Ballade des Seigneurs du Temps Jadis"', *Modern Language Review*, 55 (1960), 414–17.

'Note sur le vers 1166 du *Testament* de Villon', *Revue de Linguistique Romane*, 25 (1961), 446–7.

'Charles d'Orléans, Poète anglais?', *Romania*, 86 (1965), 434–62.

'The Rhetorical Tradition in French Literature of the Later Middle Ages', An Inaugural Lecture delivered in the University of Exeter on 17 January 1969 (University of Exeter, 24 pp.).

'An Eighteenth-Century Student of Medieval Literature: Bernard de La Monnoye', *Studies in Eighteenth-Century French Literature presented to Robert Niklaus* (University of Exeter, 1975), pp. 67–71.

'François Villon's Fifteenth Misadventure — Remarks on a Recent Book' *French Studies*, 29 (1975), 129–36.

Language and Style in the *Voyage of Saint Brendan* by Benedeit

T.D. Hemming

The masterly edition of Benedeit's poem by E.G.R. Waters embodied in its title and in the lengthy analysis of the linguistic characteristics of the text an assumption that subsequent editors and commentators have not challenged.[1] Waters, taking as his starting-point the clear evidence in the opening dedication of a connection with the court of Henry I, and in keeping with the view current at the time, took it for granted that a text written for this court in the early years of the twelfth century must be composed in the dialect peculiar to Norman England. The whole of his 76-page description and discussion of the language of the author is a model of clarity, attention to detail, and careful philological reasoning, which in fact demonstrates instead the highly distinctive, indeed unique quality of the linguistic medium in which the poem is couched. This conclusion is implicit in Waters's presentation, which is frequently punctuated by the epithets 'surprising' (e.g. pp. cxlix, clxv); 'interesting' (e.g. pp. clii, clxxvii); 'noteworthy' (e.g. pp. clii, clxvi, clxvii); 'striking' (e.g. p. clxxiv, clxxvii). The fact that he stops short of fully acknowledging and explicitly stating the very marked idiosyncracy and individuality of Benedeit's linguistic usage is itself striking, noteworthy, interesting and surprising. Given the prevailing climate of opinion at the time when he produced his edition in favour of local dialect as a dominant and determining influence, it was, it would seem, not possible even for so excellent an editor as Waters to free himself of the presupposition that a poem written in Norman England in the early twelfth century is necessarily written in Anglo-Norman. This way of looking at things posed obvious problems, the most important in the specific case of this text being the very wide differences between the language of Benedeit and that of his contemporary Philippe de Thaon. As Waters noted:

In view of the fact that both authors were *clercs*, and wrote for the same patroness, their language might have been expected to be more similar. (Introduction, p. cci)

But the problem is quickly solved:

The numerous divergencies between them point to the existence of considerable dialectal variation in Anglo-Norman during the half-century following the Conquest. (*Ibid.* p. cci)

1

Half a century after Waters, the same dialect attribution is found in the title of the edition of the poem by Ian Short and Brian Merrilees.[2] The back cover of the paperback edition states roundly that the *Voyage of Saint Brendan* is 'written in the Anglo-Norman dialect of Medieval French'. The discussion of language in the introduction (p. 10 ff.) is more cautious:

It is hardly to be expected that, in the fifty or so years that elapsed between the Norman Conquest and the composition of our poem, insular French such as that used by Benedeit should have come to differ at all significantly from its Continental stock. Indeed it is questionable whether at this early date Anglo-Norman in the sense of a separate vernacular or dialect can be said already to have existed. None the less, Benedeit's text does prove to possess certain linguistic characteristics which it is useful and necessary to describe. (p. 10)

These linguistic characteristics are, as presented by the editors, mainly phonological. They list nine significant 'divergencies from the hypothetical Continental standard' (p. 12); these are essentially the same as the first nine features identified by Waters in respect of which 'the language of the *Brendan* differs from Central French of the same period' (Waters, Introduction, p. cxcix). Waters however had already shown that virtually none of these features is distinctively characteristic of Anglo-Norman, and he summarised his findings in this regard as follows:

The use of the English words *haspe* and *rap* is probably a more conclusive sign of the insular origin of the poem than any of the phonetic or morphological features. Were it not for these words, and the depalatalisation of *l*- and *n*- mouillés, we might have conjectured the author of the poem to be a northern Frenchman whose relations with Queen Adeliza had begun even before she left her home in Brabant, and who had perhaps never visited England. (p. cc)[3]

Obviously Waters himself did not believe this to be the case, and the insular connections of the poem are not in doubt, but what does not appear to have been recognised is that the language of Benedeit cannot be made to fit at all happily and comfortably with any specific dialect, insular or continental. Certainly, it is so sharply differentiated from other contemporary and slightly later texts associated with insular court circles — most notably the works of Philippe de Thaon and *La Vie de Saint Alexis* — that it should not rightly be called the *Anglo-Norman Voyage of Saint Brendan* if, by such a designation, it is intended to imply that the text possesses certain linguistic features distinctively characteristic of the regional dialect which bears that name. Not only does the poem fail to display some of the distinctive features of Anglo-Norman; much more significantly, some of the phonological (and perhaps morphological) features that it in fact displays distance it from the Anglo-Norman dialect, as Waters himself demonstrates. On the one hand:

. . . many of the more characteristic Anglo-Norman traits are still absent from the *Brendan*, notably the confusion of *e* (*< a*) and *ie*, of *e* and *ei*, and of oral *ai* and *ei*, the suppression or introduction [. . .] of atonic *e* . . . (p. cc)

while on the other hand, unlike Philippe de Thaon, presumably as good a source of evidence for early twelfth-century Anglo-Norman as can be found, Benedeit rhymes together *-ain* and *-ein*, *n* and *n*-mouillé, and what would, in Continental French, be [y] and [u].

It is less easy to identify with confidence features of morphology and syntax which may be regarded as distinctively characteristic of Benedeit, but the following, while not necessarily being the only points, are particularly noteworthy.

Morphology

1. The extensive use of analogical feminine *-e* in adjectives and participles which etymologically do not have a distinctive feminine form, e.g. *forte* 899 (:*morte*), *grande* 240 (:*viande*), *curante* 178 etc. Short and Merrilees (p. 14) take this to be a dialectal peculiarity of Anglo-Norman, but while it is true that such forms are a feature of *later* Anglo-Norman, Waters more accurately describes them as 'somewhat surprising in so early a text'. There are very few parallels in Philippe de Thaon.

2. The free use of contracted forms of the future tense, e.g. *durat, frat*. Again Short and Merrilees regard this as an Anglo-Norman dialect trait, but Waters calls it a striking feature, and again the feature is absent from Philippe de Thaon.

3. A third 'striking feature' absent from Philippe de Thaon is the regular contraction of the imperfect subjunctive of *aveir, deveir, poeir* and *saveir* and of the corresponding ending-accented preterite forms (e.g. *oustes, doust, poust*).

Syntax

1. The sparing use of articles. (Waters, p. clxxxvii)

2. The 'surprising liberties', in Waters's phrase, which the author took with word-order. (p. cxcvi)

3. The very frequent use of elliptical constructions, and to a lesser extent of anacoluthon. Waters comments that this often accentuates the 'graphic compactness' of the narrative (p. cxcviii)

4. Parataxis. On this question there is a flat contradiction between Waters and Short and Merrilees. For Waters, parataxis is not a conspicuous feature of the poem, being much less frequent than in the *Roland*. The two more recent editors refer to the frequent use of parataxis. In this regard what is in fact distinctive about the *Brendan* is the very wide range of sentence types, from the highly paratactic:

> Deu en priet tenablement
> Cel li mustret veablement   59–60

to the very highly organised and periodic, of which the first eight lines of the poem provide a good illustration. This single sentence contains three subordinate clauses, and is so arranged that the name of the dedicatee is given honour and prominence by being placed first, while the name of the author concludes the sentence.

Stylistically as well as syntactically, the range and variety of sentence structures is obviously of considerable interest and importance.

There is no simple way of accounting for the various features of the language of the poem. In countless respects the *Voyage of Saint Brendan* stands apart, not only from contemporary insular texts but from anything else in or near the period of its composition, and the hypothesis therefore merits consideration whether in this case we may be faced with an example of idiolect, that is a usage distinctive to the author. Such a hypothesis seems to find strong support if we turn our attention from the more formal aspects of Benedeit's language to his vocabulary as embodied in this poem. Lexical matters were very fully examined by Waters in two articles in the *Modern Language Review* and again in the introduction to his edition.[4] He was concerned above all with rarities: rare and unusual words and meanings, but not, except incidentally, with their possible literary and stylistic importance. It is certainly true that in this text there are very many words not otherwise attested; words having affinities only with remote dialects and *patois*; words highly distinctive in form, words used here with meanings not otherwise attested. The whole impression given by the vocabulary is of diversity, originality and creativity, to a more marked degree than in any text before the mid-twelfth century (at the earliest), not even excluding *La Chanson de Roland*.[5]

Before considering the richness of Benedeit's poetic vocabulary, it is appropriate to mention a number of cases where stylistic considerations do not seem to apply, and where the idiolectal character of his language seems to find confirmation. These cases were not studied by Waters, and have not, I think, ever been noted hitherto. Among the earliest Old French texts, two words are found for 'day', namely *di* and *jur*. Every early text shows a decided preference for one or the other, and the distribution seems to be amenable to description and interpretation in simple terms. *Di* is very markedly predominant in the earliest texts, the *Strasburg Oaths*, the *Eulalia*, the *Vie de Saint Léger* and the Clermont-

Ferrand *Passion* narrative, but appears to become obsolete in the face of its rival *jur*, overwhelmingly dominant in the *Alexis*, the *Roland* and the works of Philippe de Thaon. Such few occurrences of *di* as are found in these texts seem to be confined to fixed phrases such as *puis cel di* or *tuz dis*. The *Brendan* stands apart, different from both groups. It alone contains a significant number of examples of both words, 20 of *di*, 21 of *jur*. Most of the cases of *di* refer to special days or feast days, but even in this respect the *Brendan* remains exceptional, for it is the only text where *di* is used with this special religious reference. There is nothing comparable in later texts either.

A slightly different case is that of words for 'thing'. The evidence of all the early texts, up to and including the *Roland*, is that *cose* is the standard term. *Nule cose* is the usual expression for 'nothing'. *Rien* is not found in the *Alexis* or the *Roland* (nor in most of the early Monuments) and is very infrequent in Philippe de Thaon. In the *Brendan, rien* is the preferred term, used freely as a substantive with such words as *une, multes, nule,* as well as the negative *ne. Chose* and *nient* also occur, but far less frequently than *rien.*

A third notable case is that of *tuer*, the colloquial character of which — indicated by its total absence from the *Roland*, and from all the early Monuments — is confirmed by its use in later twelfth-century *chansons de geste* only very sparingly and then, at first, only of animals. In the *Brendan* by contrast, *tuer* is found in the most solemn of all contexts, referring to the death of Christ:

> Puis vi que fud menez tüer   1291

as well as with reference to the suicide of Judas:

> Repentance n'en oi sage
> Ainz me tuai par ma rage   1297–8.

It is perhaps worth recalling that *di* survives in the North East, and that some later North-Eastern texts furnish instances of *rien* 'thing', so that once again Waters' tentative speculation about the possible Walloon origin of Benedeit comes to mind. But any credible explanation of the linguistic facts would have to take account of the obvious and unquestionable insular connections of the poem. The basis of Benedeit's distinctive idiolect could plausibly be an idiosyncratic mix of presumably native Walloon (or at any rate North-Eastern) and acquired Anglo-Norman (or at any rate Western) features.

On this foundation the poet builds a remarkable stylistic edifice. If we turn to what seems to be the more adventurous and creative aspect of Benedeit's vocabulary, we find a quite remarkable number of rare forms. Waters identified no fewer than 38 unique or very rare words in the poem; eleven words whose meaning in this text is otherwise unattested, and eight verbs, otherwise transitive in Old French, that are here used intransitively.[6] A few of the forms listed by Waters may be discounted for various reasons, but there remain over fifty instances, a quite remarkable figure.[7]

Of the unique and very rare words, most are etymologically transparent affixed forms or nouns derived from verbs which, even if unfamiliar, would have been readily intelligible. This is not always the case. There are, for example, several unique or rare words connected more or less closely with ships and sailing. Although John Fox has rightly pointed out[8] 'the author's evident lack of precise knowledge of seamanship' by contrast, for example, with the author of the *Vie de Saint Gilles*, Guillaume de Berneville, it would not be unjustified to apply John Fox's comment on Guillaume to Benedeit himself:

His vocabulary abounds in technical terms which he seems to accumulate for the very pleasure of using them. (p. 52)

Many of the nautical terms, rare or not, in the *Brendan*, are derived, it would seem, from Old Norse: the unique *agreies* (< *greiða*) and *beitrer* (< *beita*); *werec* (< *wreki*), *sigle* (< *segl*), *sigler* (< *segla*). The same may be true of *bat* 'boat' and *bord*, though these might equally well be straightforward Old English borrowings like *haspe* and *rap*. None the less, there are several important terms in the seafaring vocabulary of the *Brendan* which are uncontroversially accepted as deriving from Old Norse, and which therefore must have been part of the local dialect of Normandy and the Channel Islands. An earlier stratum of Germanic borrowings in this field is represented by *eschiper* (here with the exceptional meaning 'to moor'), *haler* and *mast*. Benedeit's direct knowledge of seamanship may have been limited, but his command of the relevant terminology is noteworthy and its literary exploitation seems striking. He avoids speaking of that whereof he knows nothing, yet, by the use of shipman's terms, gives an air of authenticity to what he says.

As regards the affixed forms and nouns derived from verbs, it does not seem unreasonable to regard most of these as coinages by Benedeit. Waters, though reluctant to commit himself on this question, refers to the author's 'predilection' for 'in particular' the suffixes *-eie* and *-eit*. Both are in any case quite rare in Old French, and there are no forms using these suffixes in any text earlier than the *Brendan*, nor indeed apart from this poem in any texts before the end of the twelfth century. Benedeit therefore provides at the very least the earliest attestations of these suffixes; *-eit* (< ETUM) is used to form words referring to a locality characterised by some particular natural or physical feature: *betumeit* 'boggy ground', 802 (804), cf. *betun* 'mud'; *rocheit* 'rock'; *umeit* 'damp place'; while *-eie* (< ETA) is used to form words referring to a collection of growing vegetation: *brancheie, erbeie, runceie, ruseie*. Of these, *runceie, ruseie* and *umeit* are otherwise unknown and most of the others are extremely rare.

The unusual prefixed forms and nouns derived from verbs can similarly be regarded as probable coinages by the author, but it is harder to account for the words *cisler*, *debarder* and *loreür*; Waters's comment on these seems well-judged:

> The French vocabulary of the early twelfth century is but imperfectly reflected in the extant texts of that period [. . .] The examples of *loreür* and *debarder*, [. . .] show plainly how a word can subsist for centuries, probably over a wide area, without appearing in texts. The fact that the rare words *enenz*, *cisler* and *loreür* tally with Prov. *enins*, *cisclar* and *laurador* respectively does not prove that the author of the *Brendan* had any direct connection with the South of France. (p. clxxxiv)

The fact remains that these words, like some of the sailing terms of Norse origin, do indeed occur, uniquely, in this text, and given the very diverse elements in Benedeit's language, his coinages and his novel uses of words, it is difficult to resist the conclusion that his language in this poem owes much to his own originality and creativity, that his attitude to language shows a readiness to experiment and create as well as to absorb and exploit elements from all possible sources, so as to forge a markedly individual literary medium.[9]

The literary qualities of the poem derive in no small measure from the exploitation of the resources and particularly the distinctive elements of this exceptional language, as the following illustrations show.

La nef laisent en l'*ewage*
E mangerent al rivage;
E puis chantent la cumplie
570 Od mult grant psalmodie.
Puis enz as liz tuit s'espandent
E a Jesu se cumandent.
Dorment cum cil qui sunt lassét
E tanz perilz qui unt passét.
575 Mais nepurtant a chant de *gals*
Matines dïent *ainzjurnals*,
E as *refreiz* ensemble od eals
Respunt li cors de cez oisals.

En prime main al cler soleil
580 Ast vus venant le Deu fedeil
Par qui *asen* unt cest *avei*,
E pur sun dun unt le cunrei.
E il lur ad dist: 'De vïande
Jo vus truverai plentét grande;
585 Asez averez et sanz custe
As uitaves de Pentecuste.
Puis les *travalz* estout sujurn:
Dous meis estrez ci enturn.'
Dunc prent cungé e s'en alat,
590 E al terz *di* la repairat.
Dous feiz tuz dis la semaine
Cil revisdout la cumpaine

> Cum lur ad dist, eissil firent,
> En sun seign tut se mistrent.
> 595   Quant vint li tens de lur *errer*,
> Lur nef prengent dunc a *serrer*,
> De quirs de buf la *purcusent*,
> Quar cil qu'i sunt a plein *usent*;
> Asez en unt *a remüers*
> Que estre puisset lur *baz* enters.   567–600

The first part of the extract is an abridgement of the *Navigatio*; notably, the details of the psalmody are omitted. In the second part the refitting of the boat is an authorial addition, as is the bi-weekly visit of the messenger.[10] Although this is by no means an outstanding or remarkable portion of the poem, it is reasonably representative, and there are numerous touches indicative of the author's narrative skill — abundance of circumstantial detail, dramatic presentation (*Ast vus* . . .), deft use of direct speech to enliven narrative. There is much that could be said about the style of the poem according to the traditional and well-tried methods of literary commentary, as John Fox has shown with characteristic skill,[11] but our concern here is a little different. In the extract quoted there are, in 34 lines, 14 words and phrases sufficiently unusual and remarkable to merit comment, eight of them in strong, prominent position at the rime. *Ewage*, *asen*, *avei* and *purcusent* are unique, *ainzjurnals* and *a remüers* are very rare; the meanings of *refreiz*, *travalz* and *serrer* are unusual, and the intransitive use of *usent* is not often paralleled. *Di*, as we have already seen, is part of Benedeit's idiolect, and the same is almost certainly true of *gals*, since the usual Old French term is *coq*, already attested in Philippe de Thaon. The feminine adjective *grande*, guaranteed by rime and scansion, reflects the morphological singularity of the author's language, while in respect of syntax vv. 581–2 contain a characteristically bold anacoluthon. The rimes *soleil*: *fedeil*, and *purcusent*: *usent* reflect Benedeit's distinctive phonology.

Our second illustration is part of the description of Paradise, vv. 1729 ff. For Waters, 'the poet's description . . . of the Land of Promise consists for the most part of hackneyed features' (p. 132). This may be true, but the language in which the description is couched is far from hackneyed; once again there is a dense concentration of rare and unusual words, adventurous syntactic structures and other distinctive linguistic features which give life and originality to what could have been a well-worn theme.

> Avant en vait cil juvenceals,
> 1730   Par paraïs vait ovoec eals.
> De beals bois e de rivere
> Veient terre mult plenere.
> *Gardins* est la praierie
> Qui tuz dis est beal flurie.
> 1735   Li flur süef mult i flairent
> Cum la u li piu repairent,

D'arbres, de flurs delicïus,
De fruit, d'udurs mult precïus;
De *runceie* ne de cardunt
1740   Ne de orthie n'i ad fusun;
D'arbre n'erbe n'i ad mie
Ki *süaté* ne *rechrie*.
Flurs e arbres tuz dis *chargent*
Ne pur saisun unc ne targent;
1745   Estét süef tuz dis i est,
Li fruiz de arbres e de flurs prest,
Bois repleniz de veneisun,
E tut li flum de bon peisun.
Li flum i sunt qui curent lait.
1750   Cele plentét par tut en vait:
La *ruseie* süet le mel
Par le *ruseit* qui vient del cel.
Si munt i at, cil est de or;
Si *grande* pere n'a en *tensor*.
1755   Sanz fin i luist li clers soleil,
Ne venz n'orez n'i mot un peil,
N'i vient nule nue de l'air
Qui del soleil tolget le clair
Chi ci estrat, mal n'i avrat,
1760   Ne de mals venz ja ne savrat,
Ne chalz ne freiz ne *dehaite*
Ne faim ne seit ne suffraite.   1729–62

Here the unique or very rare words are *runceie, süaté, ruseie, ruseit* and *dehaite*. The meaning of *rechrie* is the subject of a long note by Waters; the intransitive use of *charger* has few parallels in Old French; the syntax of v. 1746 and v. 1760 exercises the ingenuity of commentators, and the absence of the article before *gardins* (v. 1733) is an example of one of the 'noteworthy features' of syntax identified by Waters. Any section of the poem could provide illustrations of the same points, even if not in such convenient concentration as in the extracts quoted, and if, in respect of lexicon, the criteria were relaxed only very slightly — for we have confined our attention to words for which Tobler-Lommatzsch record fewer than four attestations — it would not be difficult to make out an even stronger case. It is not only in passages describing marvels and wonders, strange lands, exotic monsters and the like, but also, as we have seen, in much more neutral contexts that Benedeit's linguistic individuality manifests itself and contributes to the impact of his narrative.

Obviously it is difficult, if not impossible, for the modern reader to recapture any sense of the strangeness of this language; but enough has been said to show that the language of the poem is indeed strange, very different from that of Benedeit's contemporaries. The differences cannot all be accounted for, as Waters perhaps inclined to think, by the exceptional nature of the subject-matter, the author's graphic style, and his taste for realistic details. (p. clxxxiii).[12]

These qualities may account for some features of the lexicon, but can hardly have much bearing on the no less distinctive phonology, morphology and syntax. What is clear is that the poem in its specific linguistic dress was sufficiently remarkable to earn the rare tribute for a vernacular text of being translated into Latin prose and verse, and despite the unquestionable literary merits of Benedeit in terms of his imaginative gifts and his sensitive and dramatic reordering of the intermittently tedious *Navigatio*, it seems unlikely that these qualities in themselves would have been enough to warrant the accolade of retranslation into the superior Latin tongue if the language of the poem had been perceived by its hearers as unsatisfactory or distracting.[13] But surely it is possible to go further than this rather negative formulation. The strangeness, exoticism and fantastic quality of what is described and depicted is surely enhanced — and must have been enhanced for its first hearers — by the presence of unfamiliar words and meanings, by the unusual syntactic constructions, even by the strangeness of morphology and phonology. The hallmark of a literary idiolect must be its otherness from what is familiar, normal and expected, and it is difficult to imagine a more suitable work to be couched in so arrestingly singular a linguistic form. Linguistic form and literary meaning go hand in hand in this

tale of mystery and imagination which lifts people out of the humdrum of their daily lives, unfolding before their eyes the romantic and colourful spectacle of an otherworld where dreams and reality converge.[14]

Notes

1. E.G.R. Waters, *The Anglo-Norman Voyage of St. Brendan by Benedeit* (Oxford, 1928; reprint, Slatkine, Geneva, 1974). The discussion of the language occupies pp. cxxv–cci of the Introduction.

2. *Benedeit: The Anglo-Norman voyage of St Brendan*, edited by Ian Short and Brian Merrilees (Manchester, 1979); see also, by the same editors, *Le voyage de Saint-Brandan par Benedeit*, Coll. 10/18 (Paris, 1984).

3. Since Waters published his edition, L. Remacle, *Le problème de l'ancien wallon* (Liège–Paris, 1948), has shown (p. 75) that 'dans le français régional l'*l* pur s'est répandu jusque dans les Ardennes'. It cannot be regarded as a distinctive feature of Anglo-Norman.

4. E.G.R. Waters, 'Rare or Unexplained Words in the Anglo-Norman "Voyage of St. Brendan". A Contribution to French Lexicography, I', *Modern Language Review*, 21 (1926), 390–403 and 22 (1927), 28–43. The discussion of vocabulary in the introduction to his edition occupies pp. clxxix–clxxxv.

5. There are fewer than twenty *hapax* forms in the *Roland*, and some of these seem to be no more than problematic MS readings.

6. Waters discusses these cases under the rubric of vocabulary, although the point is really one of syntax.

7. For a complete list of these forms, see the Appendix to the present article, pp. 12–16, below.
8. John Fox, *A Literary History of France: The Middle Ages* (London, 1974). The discussion of the *Brendan* occupies pp. 34–42.
9. Apart from the cases discussed here, the *Brendan* also provides first attestations of a very large number of Latinisms of all kinds. Particular mention may be made of the names of precious and semi-precious stones in the description of Paradise.
10. The inclusion of the account of the refit suggests that Benedeit may have had access to some unknown source independent of the *Navigatio*.
11. Cf. in particular pp. 39–42.
12. The sentence from which this quotation is taken begins: 'Owing to the early date of the *Brendan* . . .'. It is not easy to see what the date of the poem has to do with the point that Waters is making, namely that 'the poem presents a considerable number of rare and even unique words as well as many peculiar uses of common words'. This is the case whatever the date of the poem.
13. For an account of the Latin translations of Benedeit's poem, see Waters, Introduction, pp. cv–cxxv.
14. J. Fox, *op. cit.*, p. 42.

Appendix
Unique and Rare Words and Meanings

Line references are to the edition of Short and Merrilees; references to Water's edition follow, in parenthesis, where different.

WORD	MEANING	UNIQUE	RARE	PREFIXED	SUFFIXED	DEVERBAL	ETYMOLOGY AND NOTES
ACHANT n. 1014 (1018)	tilt, lurch, 'prendre achant', capsize	X				X	<*achanter*, cf. *MLR* xxi 393.
AGREIES n. 1492 (1498)	equipment	X					<O. Norse *greiða*, cf. *MLR* xxi 394.
AORBER v. 1649 (1655)	blind	X		X			<*orbus*.
AVEI n. 581 (583)	guidance	X				X	<*aveir*, cf. *MLR* xxi 400.
AVOLST v. (AVOLDRE) 176	cover, line	X		X			<*ad + volvere*.
BEITRER v. 233	steer	X					<O. Norse *beita*, cf. *MLR* xxi 400.
BRANCHEIE n. 496 (498)	branches	X			X		*-eie* <*-eta*, collection of growing vegetation.
CELEBRIER v. 843 (845)	celebrate	X					Cf. *MLR* xxi 402.
CISLER v. 94	blow, howl	X					Cf. O. Prov. *cislar* (*fistulare + sibilare*?); *MLR* xxii 28.
CUNTRESAILIR v. 973 (977)	rise up against	X		X			Cf. Waters edition, note *ad loc.*
DEBARDER v. 1272 (1278)	squander	X					Etymology unknown. Cf. Swiss dialect *débarda*, 'dissiper ses biens, gaspiller', and v. Waters edition, note *ad loc.*
DEHAITE n. 1761 (1767)	affliction	X				X	<*dehaiter*, cf. *debait.*

Headword	Gloss	1	2	3	4	Notes
ENRUIRE v. 1125 (1129)	roar	X				<*inrugire*, cf. Waters edition, note *ad loc.*
ENTREBAT n. 1314 (1320)	interruption	X			X	<*entrebatre*.
ESTURDIER v. 1712 (1718)	make dizzy	X				Cf. *MLR* xxii 31.
EWAGE n. 567 (569)	channel		X			<*aquagium*, cf. *MLR* xxi 395.
GALESTE n. 1152 (1156)	stone, sling shot		X			<*galir*, to hurl, cf. Waters edition, note *ad loc.*
HASPES n. 686 (688)	hasp, clasp	X				<Mid. Eng. *haspe*. Cf. Waters edition, note *ad loc.*, and Short and Merrilees edition, note *ad loc.*
ISSELITES adj. 1682 (1688)	choice, exquisite	X	X			<p.p. adj. *ex-relectas or *ex-electas; cf. Waters edition, note *ad loc.* and *MLR* xxii 34.
LOREÜR n. 743 (745)	workman, servant		X			<*lauratorem, cf. *MLR* xxii 35.
NERÇUN n. 1107 (1111)	blackness	X				Cf. Waters edition, note *ad loc.*
PURCUSDRE v. 597 (599)	Sew over entirely	X		X		Cf. *MLR* xxii 36 and Waters edition, note *ad loc.*
RAPS n. 461	ropes	X				<Mid. Eng. *rap*, cf. Waters edition, note *ad loc.*
RUNCEIE n. 1739 (1745)	bramble thicket	X	X			Cf. for suffix BRANCHEIE above.
RUSEIE n. 1751 (1757)	reed bed	X	X			<Germ. *raus* + *eie* as above.
RUSEIT n. 1752 (1758)	dew	X	X			<*ros-atum*.
SÜATÉ n. 1742 (1748)	sweetness	X				<*suavitatem*, cf. Waters edition *ad loc.*

Appendix
Continued

WORD	MEANING	UNIQUE	RARE	PREFIXED	SUFFIXED	DEVERBAL	ETYMOLOGY AND NOTES
SUDUINE adj. 814 (816)	drunken	X					Etymology unknown, cf. *MLR* xxii 41.
SURPLANTER v. 1701 (1707)	set on high	X		X			Cf. *MLR* xxii 39.
SURS adv. 1384 (1390)	thereon	X					<*super* with adverbial -*s*, cf. Waters edition, note *ad loc.*
SUSPEIS n. 993 (997)	estimation, judgement	X				X	<*soupeser*, cf. *MLR* xxii 38.
SURURER v. 1604 (1610)	overstay	X		X			<**superborarre*, cf. *MLR* xxii 39.
UMEIT n. 801 (803)	damp place, boggy ground	X			X		Cf. *MLR* xxii 42.
FORMS LISTED BY WATERS BUT REJECTED HERE							
ENENZ adv. 185, 280	on board		X				Waters asserts, note to v. 185, that the adverb should be written as one word, so T.L. III, 308, but Short and Merrilees adopt *en enz*, cf. their note *ad loc.*
ENJUS adv. 1348 (1354)	below	X					Short and Merrilees adopt *en jus*, cf. *enenz* above.
ENSEIGN n. (596)	guidance						Not in MS A.
JURNALS n. 576 (578)	daybreak		X				Short and Merrilees adopt *ainzjurnals*, adj. 'pre-dawn', which is also very rare.

EXCEPTIONAL MEANINGS OF FORMS ATTESTED ELSEWHERE

AMASSET p.p.adj. 679 (681)	solid	X	Cf. *MLR* xxi 396
ASEN n. 581 (583)	instruction	X	Cf. *MLR* xxi 397.
ASENER v. 474, 506 (508) 1772 (1778)	instruct		Cf. *MLR* xxi 397.
CEU adj. 1392 (1398)	dark		
COSTIL n. 430	coast		
ESCHIPER v. 1252	moor		
FED n. 1450 (1456) 1132? (1136)	fellow		
FLAISTRE adj. 1105 (1109)	putrid		
GUERRE n. 1724 (1730) 1044 (1048)	confusion		
PRENDRE v. 1783 (1789)	comprehend		
RESORTIR v. 1694 (1700)	flash back		

OBSCURE MEANINGS

ENTAILET p.p. adj. 276	set (with precious stones)		Cf. *Waters edition, note ad loc.*

Appendix
Continued

WORD	MEANING	UNIQUE	RARE	PREFIXED	SUFFIXED	DEVERBAL	ETYMOLOGY AND NOTES
RESORTER v. 1095 (1099)	be unfaithful						Cf. Waters edition, note *ad loc.*
SERRER v. 983 (987)	propel						

NORMALLY TRANSITIVE VERBS USED INTRANSITIVELY

ABRASER 1683 (1689)	Blaze, burn vigorously						
ADENTER 902 (906)	capsize, overturn						
AMASSER 1155 (1159)	unite, solidify						
ASORBER 1650 (1656)	lose one's sight						
ASPERIR 1316 (1322)	undergo torment						
CHARGER 1743 (1749)	bear fruit						
ENBRASER 907 (911)	burn bright						
ESPANDRE 1420 (1426)	burst						

Poetic Structures in the *Couronnement de Louis*

Philip E. Bennett

The question of the structure of the *Couronnement de Louis*, or more often its lack of structure, has been a major topic of debate for a century or more. Although Joseph Bédier appeared to have resolved the basic question of unity and artistic intent,[1] even that remains open in the latest article to be published on the subject.[2] In recent years, however, more effort has gone into the analysis of the underlying structures of the poem, thematic, ideological or literary,[3] usually either presupposing or ignoring the text's inherent unity of composition, according to whether the scholar concerned is an Individualist or a Neo-traditionalist. Although this paper will, inevitably, have to take a position on the unity of the poem, this will not be its major concern; that position should derive as a natural corollary from the general argument.

That argument will look again at some of the features considered recently by Heinemann and Pickens, notably the distribution of parallel and similar segments and the organisation of the *laisse*, but it will also consider the wider implications of certain patterns of repetition and echo in those broader structures that have variously been termed episode, branch or theme, the explicit or implicit voice of a narrator in the text and the establishment of a mode for reading the text by that voice. The extent to which the subject of this paper should be considered narrative rather than poetic structures is open to debate. However, in so far as the concatenation of events and the interactive functions of 'characters' are of only secondary interest here, what follows will relate more to *poesis* than to *diegesis*.

The most obviously linked episodes in the poem, and therefore those which have been most often scrutinised in studies of this sort, are those in which Guillaume fights Corsolt and loses a slice of his nose, and in which he defends Louis's right to the empire against Gui l'Allemand. Nichols, in his typological reading of the text, points out that Guillaume's self-identification to Gui centres on the loss of his nose, and I have also indicated elsewhere[4] a number of parallels between the two episodes, which produce a similar but different typological reading. The points in question are the identity of the hill on which the duel is to take place (also referred to in Guillaume's specular discourse), the use of Charlemagne's sword Joyeuse by Guillaume in the fight, the pursuit by Gui-

17

llaume of a second enemy commander, who begs for mercy provided that his pursuer is Guillaume, and the 'procession' with which each episode ends. In considering each of these repetitions individually, one might be tempted to consider them as motifs within a normal epic mode of composition. In that case they would not be particularly significant structurally; they might have a certain effect on a modern reader of the poem, but that effect would in no way derive from the composition of the poem, being merely the product of anachronistic attitudes to art and literature on the part of the new receiver of the text. If, however, we apply, as seems totally appropriate, Duggan's remarks on the formula to the motif,[5] and can show that these repetitions are not simply an aid to oral composition, we may conclude that they are not motifs at all in the narrow sense, but do have a serious structuring function.

There is an inherent danger of circularity in this sort of argument, but in the present case we are saved from that by the nature of Guillaume's speech to Gui. It is in response to Gui's demand that he identify himself that Guillaume makes his formal statement:

> 'Voir', dit Guillelmes, 'ja le vos avrai dit:
> J'ai non Guillelme, filz le conte Aymeri,
> Cel de Nerbonne, le preu et le hardi.
> Ge doi combatre au brant d'acier forbi:
> Par droit est Rome Challe de Saint Denis,
> Et aprés lui la tendra Looÿs,
> Et ge meïsmes une bataille en fis,
> En som cest tertre, vers Corsolt l'Arrabi,
> Le plus fort homme qui de mere fust vis.
> Si me copa le nes desus le vis.'   (AB 2491–500)[6]

Although at first sight this speech is an example of the motif of the warrior identifying himself before battle, the bulk of the speech does not fit into that mould. Indeed, if we compare this speech with that made to Corsolt, we find that the two have very little in common:

> 'J'ai non Guillelmes li marchis, a non Dé,
> Filz Aymeri, le viel charnu barbé,
> Et Hermenjart est ma mere au vis cler,
> Freres Bernart de Bruban la cité,
> Frere Garin, qui tant fet a loer,
> De Commarchis Buevon le redouté,
> Frere Guibert d'Andernas le mainzné,
> Si est mes freres li chetis Aÿmer,
> Qui n'entre en loge n'en feste chevroné,
> Ainz est toz jorz au vent et a l'oré,
> Et si detrenche Sarrazins et Esclers;
> La vostre gent ne puet il point amer.'   (AB 820–31)

Because each passage is conceived in the terms of its own narrative context there is virtually no formulaic material in common between them. What there is is restricted to the allusion to Aimeri (AB 821 and 2492–3), and even this is not conceived as a formula within this poem, the common material figuring in the first hemistich in the first instance and in the second hemistich in the second instance. Moreover this genealogical information, which is the essence of the self-identification motif in other texts,[7] is found only in the B manuscripts in the speech made to Gui. Lepage refers to their being '*omis*' in all the A manuscripts,[8] but since they are equally absent in C it may be preferable to consider them as an addition in B. If this is so, then the identification motif in the Gui l'Allemand episode is reduced to a totally non-formulaic recitation by Guillaume of his previous exploit, culminating in the symbolic wound to his nose. This single piece of *mise en abyme*, whatever its origins in oral literary techniques, is used to a new purpose, that of structuring the two episodes of the poem. Consequently it also revalorises the other, frequently more formulaic, repetitions between the two episodes, so that, in Duggan's terms, they can no longer be considered as mere formulae, or, I would add, as motifs.

Turning to these other echoes, we find that they are distributed in an odd way. On each occasion the single combat takes place on a hill, and the identity of the hill in both episodes is stressed either in Guillaume's speech (AB) or by the poet-redactor (C). However, variation is introduced within this identity as a different combatant mounts the hill first on each occasion: in the Corsolt episode it is Guillaume; in the Gui l'Allemand episode it is Gui himself. The overall structure of the passage does, none the less, remain fixed:

> A dons his armour and rides to the hill —
> B observes A and calls for his armour —
> B rides to the hill —
> Verbal exchange between A and B.

This produces a relationship between the two episodes which is not that of simple repetition, or even of circularity, but rather of mirroring.

The same is true of the placing of the element of the pursuit and capture of the second enemy leader. In the Corsolt episode, this personage is Galafre, Corsolt's overlord; his capture marks the culmination of the battle for Rome, and is a prelude to Galafre's conversion and to the release of the Christian prisoners. By contrast, in the later episode, the person concerned is a subordinate of Gui l'Allemand, referred to in AB as 'Un per de Rome' (l. 2266), or as 'Dus d'Osteüse' in C (l. 2145);[9] the attack by his force on Louis's camp in the absence of Guillaume forms a prelude to the duel between Guillaume and Gui and leads immediately only to the promise of a money payment: the procession with which the Gui l'Allemand episode ends, paralleling the procession of released prisoners in the earlier episode, is here the direct consequence of the outcome of the duel. Only in this second sequence do we therefore find what might be considered to be a logical narrative structure:

> A offers a *judicium Dei*
> A specifies the consequences of the outcome
> B accepts and is victorious
> God's judgment is accepted by A and/or his supporters.

In the earlier branch the duel with Corsolt appears to have no narrative consequences despite its apparent thematic importance. Many causes for this might be posited, the most probable being a continued adherence by the poet to his model (the duel between David and Goliath in I Samuel xvii) in which a general battle between the Children of Israel and the Philistines follows the individual battle between the champions. Yet whatever the cause of this variation in structure, its effect on the wider economy of the poem is considerable. The ultimate release of the prisoners, which may be read symbolically in terms of redemption, owes more to Galafre's conversion and mock wounds than to Guillaume, his battle with a demon figure on a symbolic hill and his real wound. What might be considered as the main material of the episode has been marginalised.* Similarly, the carefully established parallels between the two episodes do not reinforce each other by the incantatory rhythm of a regular cyclic return, but become diffused in the syncopation of a series of displacements and variations:

Corsolt
1. Embassy (by Pope)
2. *Judicium Dei*
   [arming–prayer–dialogue–battle–victory]
3. Attack on Saracen camp
4. Surrender of Galafre
   [conversion–baptism]

5. Release of prisoners

Gui l'Allemand
1. Attack on Louis's camp
2. Surrender of 'per de Rome'
   [offer of money]
3. Embassy (by Gui's messenger)
4. *Judicium Dei*
   [arming–dialogue–battle–victory]
5. Procession of Romans

If we superimpose the two sequences on each other we find the following correspondences:

$$1 — 2 — 3 — 4 — 5 \quad \text{(Corsolt)}$$
$$3 — 4 — 1 — 2 — 5 \quad \text{(Gui)}$$

or, since units 1 and 2 and 3 and 4 are really subsets of larger units:

$$A — B — C \text{ (Corsolt)}$$

$$B — A — C \text{ (Gui).}$$

The tension set up by the chiasmic structure of the first two elements is resolved by the climax in the directly corresponding C sections of each sequence, which act as a kind of refrain in a song structure. In addition the first elements are linked together, in defiance of their narrative opposition, by both being associated with the theme of food.[10] This closes the circle of the poetic structure of the *chanson*, while leaving the narrative structure open and linear.

Once again, however, the use of the food motif is not simple and repetitive, and its handling has considerable implications for the structure of the poem as a whole. In the Corsolt episode the theme of food is trivial, expressed repeatedly by the Saracen's insistence that he must not be late for dinner:

> A vois s'escrie [= Corsolt]: 'Faites pais, si m'oiés:
> Les senescaus faites toz avanchier,
> Les tables metre, atorner le mangier;
> Por cel François ne l'estuet delaier:'   (C 410–13)

> 'Cuvers Franchois, or iés mal enigniés;
> A tot ton cors m'en estuet repairier,
> Car l'amiraus m'atent a son mengier;
> Mout s'esmerveille comment ai tant targié.'   (C 795–98)[11]

The frame put round the duel by Corsolt's two references to serving his belly (the second passage quoted is the immediate prelude to Guillaume's victory) tends to devalorise an enemy who, for all his claims to be pursuing a transcendent vendetta against God, never attains the terrifying demonic stature of a Gormont.[12] Thus the significance of the *judicium Dei* is further undermined by the structures within which it is set.

A similar but opposite effect is noticeable in the treatment of the first element of the Gui episode. Here the pursuit and capture of the 'per de Rome', which has no narrative consequences and which is set in weak counterpoint to the strongly valorised capture of Galafre, is given strong poetic prominence by the handling of the theme of food. This figures in two related ways. First, in relation to Louis, who is represented in camp supervising the commissariat, and who is again closely associated with the kitchen in his panic-stricken flight as the Germano-Roman forces burst in:

> Rois Looÿs i fist tendre son tref,
> Et ses aucubes et ses brahanz lever;
> Fet les cuisines et les feus alumer.   (AB 2257–9)

> Onques François ne s'i sorent gaitier,
> Tant que Romaing se sont es tres fichié:
> Chevaus en mainent, s'ocïent escuier;
> De la cuisine en portent le mangier,
> Et si ocïent le mestre despensier;
> Et Looÿs s'en vet fuiant a pié,
> De tref en autre se vet par tot mucier.   (AB 2281–7)

This repeated contamination by association marks the nadir of Louis's fortunes in the poem, scarcely surpassed by his wretched performance when Gui's ambassador arrives, and makes an unlikely prelude to the final coronation of this *Cendrillon à l'envers*. The negative treatment of the food theme in association with Louis throws out in even sharper contrast its positive use in connexion with Guillaume, as the motif of the foraging party is interwoven with it. The foraging expedition is, in fact, presented in four parallel segments starting respectively at lines AB 2260, 2264, 2291 and 2390, and thus not only provides a foil for Louis's ignominious association with food but also links the first and second elements of the Gui episode, whereas the night of celebration following Guillaume's defeat of Corsolt (AB 1164–9) marks a distinct hiatus between the two elements of that episode. This sudden intensity of repetition in a part of the poem in which, as Pickens has shown,[13] repetition is at a minimum, gives enormous poetic prominence to material whose narrative value is negligible.

Pickens has argued, from the evidence of the vastly differing proportions of repetition between the first two and the last three branches of the *Couronnement de Louis*, that there is a discrepancy in date between the two parts of the poem thus identified, and that they are of necessity by different hands. I would suggest that the careful interrelating of the structures of the Corsolt and Gui l'Allemand episodes, and the pointed use of a favourite technique from the early part of the *chanson* to give poetic and thematic prominence to material deliberately marginalised in narrative terms, tends to undermine that position. Not only is a totally atemporal cycle set up in tension against the linear narrative flow, with a complex series of repetitions and contrasts uniting the two sequences, but these repetitions themselves, and the more obvious formulaic repetitions when used, create a disjunction between the surface narrative of the text and its poetic or ideological substratum which leads to the text's ironising itself.

David Hoggan drew attention to this aspect of the text some years ago when he wrote that

> . . . le thème annoncé dans la laisse III n'est nullement celui que l'auteur veut illustrer dans sa chanson, mais bien sa contrepartie . . .[14]

and although Hoggan envisaged the *Couronnement* as a parable, which he defined as a story containing its own moral teaching, it would perhaps be preferable to view it as an enigma, whose significance the audience is required to discern through the disjunctions of the text's various levels.[15] One of the poem's most disconcerting habits is that of marginalisation, of narrative material and characters, as we have seen above, and in its *laisse* structures as analysed by Heinemann,[16] who showed that the segmental repetition used by the *Couronnement* poet made the *laisse* centrifugal rather than centripetal, with significant features falling at, or between, *laisse* boundaries. A consideration of the central diptych of the Norman Revolt and of the embracing cycle of the double coronation will reveal a remarkable consistency in the application of this principle at all levels of the text's structure.

The Norman Revolt provides an apparently linear segment within this poem built of concentric circles. Its two episodes, culminating respectively in the death of Acelin and in the imprisonment and subsequent death of Richard, are hinged around a series of five *laisses bifurquées* detailing Guillaume's campaigns in the south, three of which begin with *vers d'intonation* clearly linking the material they contain:

> Li cuens Guillelmes a la fiere personne   (AB 1999)

> Li quens Guillelmes a l'aduré corage   (AB 2004)

> Li quens Guillelmes a la chiere membree   (AB 2009)

and two of which provide a frame for the whole section:

> Trois anz toz plains fu Guillelmes le ber
> Dedenz Poitou la terre conquester;   (AB 1990–1)

> Li quens Guillelmes au cort nes le guerrier
> Vers douce France pense de chevauchier;
> Mes en Poitou lesse ses chevaliers
> Es forteresces et es chasteaus pleniers;   (AB 2022–5).

Since the second hemistich of l. 1990 and the whole of l. 2022 mimic closely the *vers d'intonation* of the *laisses* they surround, the whole sequence forms an extremely dense poetic structure, providing, once more, what Pickens would regard as abnormal verticalisation** in this part of the poem. Moreover, the poetic structure again finds itself at odds with the narrative presentation of the campaign. Only the pattern of repetitions allows us to guess the dramatic importance of this expedition of pacification, whose significance is none the less emphasised by Guillaume in his speech to Louis in *Le Charroi de Nîmes*.[17]

The superficial linearity of the post-Corsolt branches of the poem is also undermined by a series of echoes at the level of the formula, which bind features from different episodes together in achronic constellations. One such series is that which involves Louis's self-abasement before Guillaume. This gesture is presented in *laisses* 12 and 40 of AB. The former case occurs during Charlemagne's second homily to his son (in a passage heavily modified by C, but on the basis of a version that must have been very close to AB). There we read

> 'Et autre chose te vueil, filz, acointier . . .
> Que de vilain ne faces conseillier, . . .
> Mes a Guillelme le noble guerrier, . . .'
> Respont li enfes: 'Voir dites, par mon chief.'
> Il vint au conte, si li chaï as piez.
> Li quens Guillelmes le corut redrecier;
> Il li demande: 'Damoiseaus, que requiers?'   (AB 205–18).

Louis asks for Guillaume's support, which the count pledges. The scene in the abbey at Tours is designed to recall this episode. The actual formulaic echoes are only slight, and considerably transposed as to immediate context:

> Li gentis abes l'en apela premier:
> 'Filz a baron, garde ne t'esmaier:
> Vez la Guillelme, va li cheoir au pié.'
> L'enfes respont: 'Beau sire, volentiers.'   (AB 1708–11)

Louis then prostrates himself, embracing Guillaume's knees, much to the latter's increasing embarrassment as he learns who the young man kneeling before him in the gloom is. This narrative echo would seem to be of little import here, having virtually no poetic support, were it not for the fact that *laisse* 40 is a *reprise bifurquée* of *laisse* 39, which ends

> Looÿs l'ot, mout joiant en devint,
> Trusqu'au mostier ne prist il onques fin.
> Li gentis abes l'en a a reson mis:
> 'Filz a baron, ne soiez esbahiz:
> Vez la Guillelme qui sa foi vos plevi;
> Va li au pié, si li crie merci.'
> L'enfes respond: 'Tot a vostre plesir.'   (AB 1701–7)

This *segment similaire* offers not a choice of actions or attitudes on this occasion, but merely two versions, one amplified one not, of the information given to Louis by the abbot. The epic device is thus used to underscore the parallels and differences between the two episodes, and to establish them as *segments similaires* in their own right. Linear chronology is thereby abolished, and the audience is asked, in traditional epic manner, to contemplate a variety of reactions to a 'single' situation.

The same episode in the church at Tours makes a link between this branch and the beginning of the Corsolt branch. On his arrival in Rome Guillaume goes to pray and hear mass in St Peter's. After the service messengers arrive with their news of the Saracen invasion, and while Guillaume is still praying for himself and for Louis

> Li apostoiles de neant ne se targe;
> Prist un baston, si le hurte en l'espaule:
> Li quens se drece, monstre li le visage.

> XVI

> Li quens Guillelmes se dreça sor ses piez
> Et l'apostoiles l'en prist a aresnier:
> 'Hé! gentis hom, por Dieu le droiturier,
> Et quar me dites se me porroiz aidier.'   (AB 343–9)

The scene is played out again on Guillaume's arrival in Tours:

> El mostier entre, croiz fist devant son vis;
> Desus le marbre, devant le crucifi,
> La s'agenoille Guillelmes li marchis
> Et prie Dieu, qui en la croiz fu mis,
> Qu'il li envoit son segnor Looÿs.
> A tant es vos Gautier, un clerc ou vint:
> Bien reconnut Guillelme le marchis,
> Desor s'espaule li a son doi assis:
> Tant le bouta que li quens le senti.
> Li quens se dresce, si a monstré son vis:
> 'Que veus tu, frere? Garde n'i ait menti.'
> Et cil respont: 'Ja le vos avrai dit:
> Quant venuz estes secorre Looÿs,
> Fermez les huis del mostier Saint Martin.'   (AB 1662–75)

This time the similarities between the passages only serve to underscore the essential differences in tone and intention of the episodes. In Rome the pope's action tends to the violent and, by his use of a staff, to the assertion of authority. It is unclear from the context whether or not the pope was previously aware of Guillaume's presence in the cathedral, but once the count is pointed out to him he has no qualms about disturbing his devotions in the most unceremonious way. Pickens has pointed out the extent to which the pope is subject to ironic handling in the poem,[18] and this could be seen as another instance of that. However, that irony is not fully felt until we reach the abbey at Tours, where Gautier similarly taps Guillaume on the shoulder, but much more gently and considerately; moreover, and this is the key point, he comes not to cut across Guillaume's devotions but as an answer to his prayers. The only formulaic echoes are those of ll. 345–6 and 1671, and these are both discreet and of comparatively little significance; it is unlikely that they alone would trigger a sufficient act of memory in the audience. However, the overall pattern within the motif of prayer in a particularly sacred place for the safety of Louis — interruption by tap on shoulder — conversation would provide enough parallels to link the episodes in the listener's mind, while the subsequent bifurcations would underscore the differences, valorising the worthy clerk and further devalorising an already discredited pope. Once again the structure of the poem establishes a circle, but, as with the other cyclic structures we have seen, this one includes an inversion, this time within the narrative material affecting our attitude to the characters.

The all-embracing cycle that encloses the others we have been observing is that formed by the double coronation. Pickens[19] has expressed the opinion that, along with the killing of Corsolt, the successful coronation of Louis at Aix is 'obviously' one of the most important elements of the poem. However, if we look closely at the episodes concerned we may be led to query that proposition. The first episode of the poem in redaction AB covers thirteen *laisses* and 273 lines. Of these, one, *laisse* 13, deals with Guillaume's leave-taking, three (*similaires*) are given to the voice of the narrator by way of theoretical prologue, two *laisses parallèles* establish the magnificence of the assembly at Aix for the benediction of the chapel and the institution of the court of justice, in the course of which Louis is crowned, and no fewer than six parallel *laisses* deal with admonitions from Charles on the duties of kingship and questions of inheritance, wardship and regency. The coronation occupies just eight lines at the end of the long *laisse* 8:

> Voit la coronne qui desus l'autel siet:
> Li quens la prent sanz point de l'atargier,
> Vient a l'enfant, si li assiet el chief:
> 'Tenez, beau sire, el non de Dieu del ciel,
> Qui te doint force a estre justisier!'
> Voit le li peres, de son enfant fu liez:
> 'Sire Guillelmes, granz merciz en aiez:
> Vostre lignages a le mien essaucié.'   (AB 142–9)

Even allowing for the mild parallelism of ll. 142 and 147 this gives scant emphasis by its poetic means to such a major event, which provides the incipit to the poem in five manuscripts.

A similar puzzle exists in respect of the coronation in Rome with which the poem closes. Here we do have two formal *segments parallèles*, but they only serve to emphasise the marginalisation of the events narrated:

LXI

> Par dedenz Rome fu Guillelmes li frans
> Prent son segnor tost et isnelement,
> En la chaiere l'asiet de maintenant,
> Sel corona del barnage des Frans.

La li jurerent trestuit le serement.
Tiex li jura qui ne le tint neant,
Com vos orroiz ainz le soleil couchant.

LXII

Par dedenz Rome fu Guillelmes le ber,
S'a Looÿs son segnor coroné:
De tot l'empire li a fet seürté.
Lors s'apareille et pense de l'errer.　　　(AB 2618–27).

From this point there is a bifurcation detailing the failure of Louis to remain established in his capital in the face of the revolts predicted in l. 2623. Moreover, the *vers d'intonation* emphasise Guillaume's prowess, while the coronation is as rushed as it was in Aix, and, if this second coronation with its references to the empire is intended to recall Charlemagne's speech on the subject in ll. 72–9, thereby closing the circle of the poem completely, its collocation at the end of the Gui l'Allemand episode merely serves once more to ironise the king and to marginalise its purported material. Redaction C, for its part, expands the second coronation scene and increases Louis's importance by having him create a new pope to replace the one who died at the start of the Gui l'Allemand episode. This breaks the cycle, and achieves a genuine climax before the disasters that await back in France. However, Hoggan has shown that this new ending in C is due to material considerations within the text of C itself,[20] and that the AB version most probably represents the intentions of the archetype.

The *Couronnement de Louis* thus presents us with a structure of two concentric circles (Coronation — Coronation and Corsolt — Gui l'Allemand) which themselves surround an apparently linear unit (Norman Revolt). However, the 'centre' of the poem, and of the Norman Revolt episode itself, falls not at the mid-point but approximately three-quarters of the way through both poem and branch, at least in Redaction AB, where the eccentric pivot of highly verticalised *laisses* falls at ll. 1990–2025. In redaction AB the poem has 2670 lines and the Norman Revolt occupies ll. 1368–2200; the exact three-quarters points therefore come at l. 2003 and l. 2016 respectively. This effect is somewhat dissipated in redaction C, which is abbreviated at the beginning and amplified at the end, so that the hinge falls at ll. 1769–815 out of 2715 for the whole poem, in which the Norman Revolt occupies ll. 1060–2041. This displaces the pivot to nearer the golden section of the whole poem, but leaves it just under three-quarters of the way through the Norman Revolt. Furthermore the pivot is much less verticalised than in AB, but, as with other modifications in C the parallelisms of ll. 1769/1810 and 1770/1811, as well as other internal narrative features, reveal its dependence on a model from which AB also derives. We can therefore assume with some confidence that AB reflects the intentions of the archetype reasonably closely, and that the disruption of the orderly cyclic structure is not accidental.

I have referred above to Pickens's suggestion that a diminution of repetition, and thus of 'lyric' verticality, at the end of the Corsolt branch indicates multiple authorship. However, the carefully planned external repetitions with significant variations which link the branches after this point, largely replacing internal repetition in statistical count (while this is still used intensively at significant moments to support, or undermine, the apparent message of the external repetition) transfer verticality onto a broader textual plane affecting the poem as a whole rather than individual elements of the poem. This would tend to indicate the unity of composition of the poem as it has come down to us.

It is also notable that these repetitions and cycles tend to extend to narrative elements and characters that marginalisation which Heinemann has noticed in *laisse* structure. Not only are Louis, Guillaume and the pope marginalised and ironised at various points, but so are Charlemagne, Galafre, Gaifer and his daughter and the sacred sword Joyeuse. And so above all is what purports to be the essential material of the poem: the coronation of Louis. The text thus presents itself as an enigma, at odds with itself, and, as Hoggan has pointed out, at odds with its own ideology as stated in the prologue. Like *La Chanson de Roland, Le Couronnement de Louis* offers no solution to the battle against evil, which it sees in political terms rather than in the eschatological terms of the *Roland*; that, like everything else in the poem, is cyclic. However, by its production of an intricate pattern of self-referential cycles, *Le Couronnement de Louis* does invite its audience to cogitate on the problem of political instability and royal inadequacy within a providential order of established legitimate kingship and feudal loyalty.

Notes

*Marginalise/marginalisation are here used to mean the relegation to narrative insignificance of a symbolically important feature or to symbolic insignificance of an important narrative feature. They are the macrostructure equivalents of Heinemann's 'principe centrifuge', by which individual narrative elements are related to the structure of the isolated *laisse* in his article 'L'art de la laisse dans le *Couronnement de Louis*', cited below, note 3.

**Verticalisation/verticalise/verticality are here used in the sense attributed to them by Pickens, whereby repetitive, atemporal, lyric elements are considered as existing on a vertical axis cutting perpendicularly through the horizontal axis of chronologically sequential narrative:

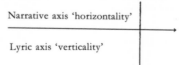

Narrative axis 'horizontality'

Lyric axis 'verticality'

See R.T. Pickens, 'Art épique et verticalisation', cited below, note 2.

1. J. Bédier, *Les Légendes épiques* (Paris, Champion, 1908), Vol. 1, Chap. VII.
2. R.T. Pickens, 'Art épique et verticalisation: problèmes narratifs dans le *Couronnement de Louis*', *Vox Romanica*, 45 (1986), 116–49.

3. R. Blumenfeld-Kosinski, 'Praying and Reading in the *Couronnement de Louis*', *French Studies*, 40 (1986), 385–92.

J.J. Duggan, 'Formulas in the *Couronnement de Louis*', *Romania*, 87 (1966), 315–44.

J. Frappier, 'Les thèmes politiques dans le *Couronnement de Louis*', in *Mélanges de linguistique romane et de philologie médiévale offerts à M. Maurice Delbouille*, ed. Jean Renson (Gembloux, Duculot, 1964), Vol. 2, 195–206.

E.A. Heinemann, 'Sur l'art de la laisse dans le *Couronnement de Louis*', in *Charlemagne et l'épopée romane* [Actes du VII⁰ Congrès international de la Société Rencesvals: Liège, 28 août–4 septembre 1976], ed. M. Tyssens and C. Thiry (Liège, Presses de l'Université, 1978), 383–91.

D.G. Hoggan, 'L'unité artistique du *Couronnement de Louis*', *Romania*, 89 (1968), 313–39.

Huguette Legros, 'La réalité sociale dans *Le Couronnement de Louis*', in *Guillaume d'Orange and the Chanson de geste*, ed. W.G. van Emden and P.E. Bennett (Reading, Société Rencesvals: British Section, 1984), 67–73.

Stephen Nichols, Jr, 'Sign as (Hi)story in the *Couronnement de Louis*', *Romanic Review*, 71 (1980), 1–9.

David P. Schenck, '*Le Couronnement de Louis*: a Mythic Approach to Unity', *Romanic Review*, 69 (1978), 159–71.

4. Philip E. Bennett, 'Guillaume d'Orange, Fighter of Demons and Harrower of Hell', in *Myth and Legend in French Literature, essays in honour of A.J. Steele*, ed. K.R. Aspley, D. Bellos and P. Sharratt (London, MHRA, 1982), 24–46.

5. Duggan, *art. cit.*, p. 319.

6. *Les Rédactions en vers du Couronnement de Louis*, édition avec une introduction et des notes par Yvan G. Lepage [TLF 261] (Geneva and Paris, Droz, 1978). All quotations are from this edition. My analysis is normally based on the AB redaction, although C is invoked where there are distinct signs of significant innovation in the ancestor(s) of the extant AB manuscripts.

7. The motif of a warrior identifying himself to an enemy can be inserted at a variety of points in the combat motif. It can be very simple, as in *Fierabras*, where Oliver identifies himself to his Saracen opponent prior to their duel:

> 'J'ai nom Olivier, si sui de Gennes nés,
> Si sui compains Rollant et uns des .xii. pers.'
> (*Fierabras*, ed. A. Kroeber and G. Servois [APF 4], ll. 706–7)

or more fully developed, as when Guillaume mutters his identity, as much to reassure himself as to warn Harpin, in *Le Charroi de Nîmes*:

> 'Por ce, s'ai ore mes granz sollers de vache
> Et ma gonele et mes conrois si gastes,
> Si ai ge non Guillelmes Fierebrace,
> Filz Aymeri de Narbonne, le sage,
> Le gentil conte qui tant a vasselage.'
> (*Le Charroi de Nîmes*, ed. D. McMillan (Paris, Klincksieck, 2nd ed., 1978), ll. 1336–40).

The most elaborate version comes in *Le Roman d'Hector et Hercule* where, just before he dies, Hercules elicits Hector's identity in a series of questions and answers covering 122 lines (1135–256). However, the nub of the motif remains the identification of the young hero's parentage:

> L'enfant repont: 'Le nom de moi
> Nen voi a vos tenir secroi.
> J'ai nom Hector, niés Laumedon,
> Por la qiel mort ou vos tenchon.'
> 'Adonc es filz le roi Priam . . .'
> (*Le Roman d'Hector et Hercule*, ed. J. Palermo [TLF 190] (Geneva, Droz, 1972), ll. 1239–43).

The motif takes a different form in *Gormont et Isembart*, when Hugelin identifies himself to

Gormont by reference to a previous exploit, in which he appears to have used magic to ridicule Gormont (*Gormont et Isembart*, ed. A. Bayot [CFMA 14**], ll. 241–6). The change in the motif may be explained by Hugelin's apparent Other World origins, see Philip E. Bennett, 'Le personnage de Hugelin dans *Gormont et Isembart*', *Marche Romane*, 29, 3–4 (1979), 25–36. Nevertheless, the motif survives into romance, where we find it, for instance, in Chétien's *Yvain*:

> 'Ja mes nons ne vos iert celez
> Gauvains ai non, fiz le roi Lot.'
> (Chrestien de Troyes, *Yvain*, ed. T.B.W. Reid (M.U.P., Manchester, 1942), ll. 6266–7).

8. *Ed. cit.*, p. 389.
9. The author of *Le Charroi de Nîmes* extrapolates this incident and makes of it a totally separate branch, that of the 'grant ost Oton' (*ed. cit.*, ll. 213 ff.). Although it is now accepted that the *Charroi* is not a reflection of an older, lost *Couronnement* (see J. Frappier, *Les Chansons de geste du cycle de Guillaume d'Orange* (Paris, SEDES, 2nd ed., 1964), Vol. 2, 53–7 and 203–4), it is noteworthy that the *Charroi* also suppresses all mention of Galafre. In this way any sense of the structure of the poem supposedly 'quoted' is lost.
10. Schenck, *art. cit.*, and 'Le mythe, la sémiotique et le cycle de Guillaume', in *Charlemagne et l'épopée romane*, 373–82, depicts the motif of food as one of the positive poles (regeneration-civilisation) in the semiotic structuring of the *Couronnement de Louis* and other poems of the cycle. As we see here, food is an ambivalent factor, negative in relation to Corsolt and Louis, positive in relation to Guillaume.
11. The A manuscripts have innovated at these points; I have quoted the C redaction since its reading is supported by the B manuscripts.
12. J. Györy, 'Epaves archaïques dans *Gormont et Isembart*', in *Mélanges offerts à René Crozet à l'occasion de son soixante-dixième anniversaire*, ed. P. Gallais and Y.-J. Riou (Poitiers, 1966), 675–84.
13. Pickens, *art. cit.*, and 'Comedy, History and Jongleur Art in the *Couronnement de Louis*', *Olifant*, 11 (1986), 207–8 n.6.
14. Hoggan, *art. cit.*, p. 317.
15. For the model of this type of text in Old French see Leigh A. Arrathoon, 'Jacques de Vitry, the Tale of Calogrenant, *La Chastelaine de Vergi*, and the Genres of Medieval Narrative Fiction', in *The Craft of Fiction, Essays in Medieval Poetics*, ed. Leigh A. Arrathoon (Rochester Mi., Solaris Press, 1984), 281–368.
16. Heinemann, *art. cit.*, 389–90.
17. *Ed. cit.*, ll. 157–61.
18. Pickens, 'Comedy, History and Jongleur Art', 209–18.
19. Pickens, 'Art épique . . .', 140–2.
20. D.G. Hoggan, 'L'"isotope C38" dans la composition des poèmes du cycle de Guillaume', in *Société Rencesvals, VIe Congrès international (Aix-en-Provence, 29 août–4 septembre, 1973) Actes*, ed. J. Subrenat (Aix-en-Provence, Université de Provence, 1974), 561–82.

'En ensivant la pure verité de la letre': Jean de Vignay's translation of Odoric of Pordenone

D.A. Trotter

Jean de Vignay's translation of Odoric of Pordenone's account of his journey to Cathay in the early fourteenth century is one of two extant contemporary French versions. The other, slightly later version, by Jean le Long, abbot of Saint-Bertin, survives in seven manuscripts and was edited by Henri Cordier at the end of the last century.[1] There are two manuscripts of Jean de Vignay's unpublished translation, Rothschild 3085 in the Bibliothèque Nationale in Paris and Royal 19.D.I in the British Library. Neither seems to be the original, but they have enough in common for a common exemplar to be postulated at some stage in the transmission of the text. I am currently preparing an edition for the Exeter French Texts series. What I should like to do in this paper is to look at Jean de Vignay's translation *as a translation*, comparing it briefly with some of his other efforts in this domain, and concentrating, in particular, on the extent to which the style of the finished product has been influenced — lexically, semantically and, above all in this case, syntactically — by the fact that the work is a translation. No doubt this sounds rather banal; it is always true, to some extent, of the translator's craft, where interference from the source language is an occupational hazard. But it is particularly true of translation as Jean de Vignay and some, at least, of his contemporaries, conceived it.

A fundamental, although frequently neglected, problem when discussing medieval translation arises from the difficulty of determining which manuscript the translator used. Odoric of Pordenone's travelogue evidently, and from our point of view regrettably, enjoyed considerable popularity throughout the Middle Ages: in addition to the two French translations, it was also rendered into German and Italian. At least sixty Latin manuscripts have survived, there is no real critical edition, and even the preliminary classification of the manuscripts has never been satisfactorily completed. The consensus, in most cases based, one suspects, on a good deal of second-hand information, seems to be that the original (and therefore, naturally, lost) text was dictated by Odoric on his return from the Far East in 1330 to one William of Solagna, whose autograph copy, formerly, but

31

no longer, identified with a manuscript preserved in Assisi, is also lost. In 1340, a second redaction was written by Henry of Glars (Glatz, now Kłodzko, on the border between Poland and Czechoslovakia), in Prague. This initial division of the texts, which does not by any means account for all of them, is almost wholly based on the colophons of the manuscripts, and whether they mention William or Henry. There are probably two other redactions, that represented by the text published by the English scholar Richard Hakluyt in 1599, and that which is the basis of the so-called 'Minor Ramusian' text, published, posthumously, from the papers of the Italian scholar Ramusio in Venice in 1583. The relationship of these redactions to the two principal redactions is not clear. All that we can say with any certainty at all is that Jean de Vignay follows the earliest of the four versions, that attributed to William of Solagna, for the very simple reason that he translates the colophon. This redaction is further divided by the editor of the best text of Odoric into four sub-redactions, and a comparison of Jean de Vignay's version and the manuscript variants provided in the Latin text suggests that it is possible to identify which sub-redaction he was using, but also, unfortunately, to establish with a reasonable degree of certainty that the Latin manuscript used is not one of those which has been published. Whether it still exists is uncertain.[2] In what follows, the expression 'the Latin original' is, therefore, to be treated with suitable scepticism.

Jean de Vignay[3] is the author of eleven extant translations, and a lost *Roman d'Alexandre*, also probably a translation, spanning the period from about 1320 to the mid-1350s. Most of his prologues tend to be euphuistic eulogies of his royal patrons (he worked for Philippe VI de Valois as well as for Jeanne de Bourgogne) rather than cogent summaries of translation theory, but there are two laudably explicit exceptions. These are the prologues to his translations of Vegetius's *De re militari* and of *Les Enseingnemens de Theodore Paliologue*. The former dates from the earlier period of his prolific career (*circa* 1320); the latter, a French version of a largely lost Byzantine Greek military treatise of the early fourteenth century, is a later work, dating from somewhere between 1335 and 1350. Both texts have recently been published in excellent editions.[4] The prologue to Jean de Vignay's Vegetius reveals the translator's policy in no uncertain terms:

Mes por ce que li livres est en latin liquels n'est pas communement entenduz des chevaliers, a il esté ausi comme mis en nonchaloir. Et ie, sanz nule presumpcion, par commandement, veil metre le dit livre en françois selonz ce que je porré en ensivant la pure verité de la letre. Et se par aventure ie ne sai ensi bien trover le françois plenemant com mestiers seroit au droit entendement du livre, je pri le lector qu'il m'ait escusé et debonerement amende le mesfet, quar ce n'est pas granz los de reprendre autrui fet s'en ne velt amender ce qui est meins bien fet. De metre l'uevre en rime ne me veil entremetre, mes la verité pure sivre selonc la letre. Car si comme l'en dit et maintes foiz avient, en oevre mise en rime sovent faus entrevient.[5]

Two manuscripts of this text (both in Cambridge) add, after the *explicit*, 'Ci fenist le livre Flave Vegece, [. . .], translaté de latin en françois, mot a mot, selonc le latin'. It has been suggested[6] that Jean de Vignay's ' "truth" is insight into realities signified by linguistic signs' rather than literal truth, but neither the additional comment in these manuscripts, nor, indeed, the standard of the translations themselves, supports so sophisticated an interpretation of the translator's own view of his task. According to the editor of the Vegetius translation,[7] 'le programme de traduction littérale annoncé au commencement de la traduction, a été suivi de façon rigoureuse presque partout dans le Végèce'; Claude Buridant has written of a 'modelage étroit sur l'original' and of a 'mimétisme étroit'.[8] Not that Jean de Vignay's preliminary observations are devoid of trite cliché. The observation about the inherent mendacity of rhyme in the penultimate sentence is familiar as a restatement of the 'nus contes rimés n'est verais' *topos*,[9] and, indeed, paradoxically enough, the whole of the last section of this passage is written in Alexandrines:[10]

> quar ce n'est pas granz los de reprendre autrui fet
> s'en ne velt amender ce qui est meins bien fet.
> De metre l'uevre en rime ne me veil entremetre,
> mes la verité pure sivre selonc la letre.
> Car si comme l'en dit et maintes foiz avient,
> en oevre mise en rime sovent faus entrevient.

Translation of a text of this sort has a didactic and utilitarian function: to make available to the *chevaliers* (who can perhaps read, but not Latin) a useful text which would otherwise be inaccessible to them. Similar sentiments are expressed in the prologue to *Les Enseingnemens de Theodore Paliologue*:

A la tres excellent, tres poissant et tres noble majesté royaul et filz d'Eglise tres crestien, Phelippe, par la grace de Dieu roy des Frans et prince tres soverain sur tous les autres [. . .] Et pour ces choses et aultres pluseurs, et meïsmement pour la cause que le plus dez nobles hommes, et especialment hommes d'armes, ne sont pas communement lectrez, ay je mis le dit livre de latin en franceois, affin que il soit plus entendible aux nobles hommes d'armes qui ne sont pas lectrez. . .[11]

To be *entendible* to men-of-arms, the treatise must be in French, since they are not *lectrez*, with, again, the suggestion that they might be able to read French but not Latin (this is, of course, one of the possible meanings of the Latin equivalent *litteratus*[12]). There is not the same emphasis on literal translation — indeed, the end of the prologue to the *Enseingnemens* specifically admits that the author has 'delaissié plusieurs choses, tant pour cause de briefté comme pour ce que y ne touchoient point au fait dez armes ne de guerre'.[13] Absence of appropriate theoretical statements notwithstanding, a similar 'extrême fidélité au latin' is nonetheless detectable in this translation.[14]

No such *profession de foi* accompanies the translation of Odoric of Pordenone. A number of Latin manuscripts indicate[15] that Odoric himself died in 1331, and this note is translated in both the manuscripts of Jean de Vignay's version. The Royal manuscript has an illustration, preceding this text, in which the translator is shown presenting his book to Philippe VI; a similar illustration appears at the beginning of the translation by Jean de Vignay of Gervase of Tilbury's *Otia Imperialia*, the only other text in the Rothschild manuscript. It is possible that the translation of Odoric was executed at the same time as Jean de Vignay's version of the crusading manual or *Directorium ad passagium faciendum*, probably produced at Philippe's request after he had been presented with the Latin text of this work in 1332[16] and before he abandoned his crusading plans in 1334. This translation appears, dated 1333, in the Royal manuscript. Notionally at least, Odoric's account is of a missionary expedition: he claims to be — in Jean de Vignay's translation — 'couvoitant de aler as parties des mescreans, si que je feïsse aucuns fruis des ames' (*P*, f. 207ᵉ a). It is clear, in fact, that the narrative was popular not because of this element (which, apart from a lengthy account of the martyrdom of four Franciscans off Bombay in 1321, is promptly forgotten) but because of the 'mout de grans choses et merveilleuses' (*ibid.*) with which the author regaled a public avid for more Marco Polo-type literature. It is no accident that Odoric and Marco Polo are frequently found in the same manuscripts (including Royal 19.D.I). Jean de Vignay's translation of Odoric is, in short, a plausible companion volume to his translation of the *Directorium*.

It has been observed of Jean de Vignay that 'ses meilleures traductions sont celles où le texte latin est simple et clair'.[17] A less charitable way of putting this would be to say that his translations are at their best when the original Latin is easy and when following it slavishly does not produce too stilted a French text. Most of us would doubtless find the same was true of our own translations. Odoric's Latin, or that of his amanuensis, is far removed from the complexity of, for example, Vegetius, and the translation is correspondingly better. Perhaps because the original Latin owes something to its author's Romance vernacular (although this would need further investigation), direct, word-for-word translation produces, most of the time, an acceptable result. Some idea of how literal the translation is may be gathered from the following short excerpt, chosen at random (it is from Chapter IX, concerned with Malabar, which Odoric calls Minibar). Given below is, first, the French text and, second, the Latin text, with variants when these appear closer to the French. The base manuscript for the latter is *P*, the Rothschild manuscript, with variants from the Royal manuscript (*L*).

[*P*, f. 215ᵛ b] Pour ce que nous sachon (*L*: sachons) comment le poivre est eu, vous devez savoir que en .i. empire, la ou je alai par mer, Minibar par non (*L*: qui a non Minibar), et en nul autre partie du monde que l'en sache, il ne croist habondaument, fors que la (*L*: Quer poivre ne croist si habondaument en nulle autre partie du monde tant comme la). Et le bois certes en quoi le poivre croist contient bien en soi .xviij. jornees. Et en ce bois sont .ij. citez, l'une par non (*L*: l'une qui a non) Flandrine et l'autre a non Cingule (*L*: et l'autre Cingule). En ceste cité Flandrine (*L*: En la cité de Flandrine) aucuns des habitans sont juis et les autres crestiens. Et entre ces .ij. citez est touzjors aussi comme [f. 216^{r}a] bataille (*L*: est touzjours bataille) de l'une a (*L*: et de) l'autre, en tel maniere que les crestiens seurmontent touzjours et vainquent les juis.

The Latin text reads as follows (manuscript sigla follow those in Van den Wyngaert's edition):

Ut autem sciatis (*CY*: sciamus) quomodo habeatur piper, sciendum est quod in imperio quodam, ad quod aplicui nomine Minibar, nascitur ipsum piper, et non est in aliqua parte mundi nisi ibi (*B*: Et non est illo excepto ita bonum in aliqua parte mundi). Nemus enim in quo nascitur ipsum piper (*C omits* et non . . . piper) continet in se bene 18 dietas, et in ipso nemore sunt due civitates, una nomine Flandrina, altera vero Çinglin (*B*: Cingalum). In ista Flandrina habitancium aliqui sunt iudei, aliquo vero christiani. Inter has duas civitates bellum (*Y*: bellum intestinum) semper habetur, ita tamen quod christiani semper superunt et vincunt iudeos.[18]

Jean de Vignay is evidently still following his own precept in the Vegetius prologue, 'la verité pure sivre selonc la letre'. This is especially true of MS *P*, visibly a clumsier rendering — whatever the putative original may have contained. In view of the translator's own views on the virtues of literal translation, this is one reason for concluding that it is the more reliable guide to what he himself would have written. The inferior translation (by our standards) is probably the more authentic text. This tendency for *L* to be a freer rendering is found throughout the work, and is particularly apparent in those cases where the *P* version, and perhaps the original translation, is at its most literal. A number of the more striking cases of this phenomenon will form the subject-matter of the remainder of this paper, before some tentative general conclusions are drawn regarding the nature and role of a translation which adopts this form. The numbers in what follows refer to the appendix to this paper.

There are several straightforward errors in Jean de Vignay's translation (1, 2). In the first of these, the Latin text describes the female Chaldeans as '(ferrentes) solum unam (*BY add*: vilem) interulam' (Hakluyt and a related manuscript have 'camisiam'). The French text of *L* reads 'une seule vielle chemise', where *P* has the correct 'vile'; *L* is obviously wrong. Comment is being passed on the quality of the ladies' apparel rather than its antiquity. It is difficult to see how this error could have crept into the Latin text, or indeed at the stage of the translation from Latin to French, and it presumably derives from the process by which *L* itself was copied. The second example, where the error has survived in both French manuscripts, concerns what the Latin text calls 'unum pedem faxiolorum'. Jean de Vignay thinks that a 'faciolus' is a type of tree, and translates 'un arbre qui est apelé "faciolus"'. In fact, what is apparently meant is a bundle or stack of twigs (in the event, from the *Ocimum sanctum*, a species of basil much revered, we are told, by the Hindus). The exact meaning of the expression is not absolutely clear, but it cannot easily refer to a singular tree. Here, apparently, the error goes back to the translator himself. The best example of the pitfalls of literal translation is the rendering of the Great Khan (Canis Magnus, Canis Grandis) as 'le Grant Chien' (*passim*; 3–10 are merely examples). In the absence of any evidence that Jean de Vignay actually thought that the Khan resembled some sort of monocephalous oriental Cerberus, we must conclude that this is a translation error. It is a remarkably consistent one, only partly redeemed by *L*'s sporadic awareness (5, 9) that another possible name was 'le Grant Caen', which is presumably a phonetic rather than an etymological version of the ruler's title. In the same vein, perhaps, is the calque whereby the Latin 'de Foro Julii', Odoric's place of origin (Friuli), becomes the quite meaningless 'du Marchié Julien' in Jean de Vignay's translation.[11]

Translations are an obvious route both for loan-words and for semantic borrowings, whereby the (in this case) French word regresses, as it were, to its Latin meaning.[19] In the prologue to the early fourteenth-century *Psautier de Metz*, a fascinating and linguistically perspicacious document, loan-words are cited as something to which translators inevitably have recourse:

il n'est nulz, tant soit boin clerc ne bien parlans romans, qui lou latin puisse translateir en romans quant a plusour mos dou latin; mais couvient que, per corruption et per diseite des mos françois, que en disse lou romans selonc lou latin, si com: *iniquitas* 'iniquiteit', *redemptio* 'redemption', *misericordia*, 'misericorde' . . .[20]

The last-mentioned word, *misericorde*, occurs in Jean de Vignay's version of Odoric (24). *Misericorde* is, of course, found in texts which are not translations, but the point is that, here, it has patently been introduced as a result of the presence of the word *misericordiam* in the Latin. Sometimes the translator, or the scribe of one of the two manuscripts, seems aware of this, as the variant reading of *L* reveals in another case (22): *P* has 'Et ainssi par ceste maniere en .i. jour naturel'. *L* has felt the need to gloss the expression *jour naturel*, which is a literal translation of the original 'in una die naturali', as, 'en .i. jor naturel, c'est assavoir jour et nuit'. The expression, however, is attested elsewhere too.

There are a number of meanings of words which are *not* attested elsewhere, or at least have not been recorded in the dictionaries: *incredible* (23), first recorded (in this sense of 'unbelievable') in Deschamps, some 50 years later; *combien* to refer to distance ('il font illec .i. signe en la voie ou il font ce qui est dit devant, si que il sachent combien il sont venuz (16)', a very literal translation of the Latin 'ut sciant quantum processerunt'); *par especial* (17) to translate 'in speciali', i.e. 'apart', 'individual' (referring to individually-owned houses); *respondre* as a translation of the Latin *correspondere* in the phrase (13) 'aussi comme tout le monde respont a cele cité pour marcheandises, where 'respont a' translates 'correspondet' in the Latin: note that MS *L* again renders the Latin more freely ('Quer tout le monde vient a cele cité pour toutes marcheandises'; cf. also 14, where *L* has 'contient' and *P* 'se respont'). In all these cases, the immediate proximity of the Latin equivalent has certainly facilitated, if not engendered, the semantic borrowing which has occurred. Taken to extremes, the use of loan-words or semantic borrowing would obviously run the risk of turning the exercise of translation into one of pointless transliteration; Di Stefano has rightly pointed out that

ou bien le lecteur connaît le mot, sous sa forme latine ou dans la réécriture française, peu importe, et il n'a pas besoin de la médiation du traducteur, ou bien cette médiation est d'un rendement nul.[21]

Jean de Vignay is aware of the problem, which is why he occasionally glosses his own translation; going still further, Pierre Bersuire, in the mid-fourteenth century, prefaces his translation of Livy with a 70-word glossary of the neologisms he feels obliged to use.[22] Fortunately, the nature of the vocabulary which Jean de Vignay is confronted with does not produce a problem of the type identified by Roger Bacon, writing of the difficulties involved in translating logic into one's mother tongue:

Certe logicus non poterit exprimere suam logicam si monstrasset per vocabula linguae maternae; se oporteret ipsum nova fingere, et ideo non intelligeretur nisi a seipso.[23]

It is in the realm of syntax rather than that of vocabulary that Jean de Vignay's translation of Odoric is in greatest danger of being comprehensible only to its author, and of emerging, in the words of the translator of the *Psautier de Metz*, as neither 'latin boin ne romans, mais aucune foiz moitieit latin moitieit romans'.[24] 'Mot a mot, selonc le latin', is apt to mean just that; in medieval terms, his translation is resolutely *ad litteram* rather than *ad sensum*, and disentangling the *sensus* from his convoluted and Latinate *littera* can, at times, be something of a challenge. Not that contemporaries were oblivious of the risks of syntactic interference: Jean d'Antioche, in the prologue to his late-thirteenth-century translation of the pseudo-Ciceronian *Rhetorica ad Herennium*, observes that the translator

ne pot mie porsiure l'auctor en la maniere dou parler, car la maniere dou parler au latin n'est pas semblable generaument a cele dou françois, ne les proprietez des paroles ne les raisons d'ordener les araisonemenz et les diz du latin ne sont pas semblables a celes dou françois.[25]

Some syntactic influence, of course, is, like the influence of Latin vocabulary, fortuitous, in the sense that the French construction which the adjacent Latin apparently provokes may well not be, strictly speaking, a Latinism, since it is attested independently elsewhere. We would do well to heed Charles Brucker's warning on the subject of syntactic calques:

il convient de se montrer prudent avant de taxer de calque telle ou telle tendance latinisante

[. . .] la traduction, au moyen âge, du latin en français a un effet de grossissement, à deux titres au moins; d'une part, le traducteur qui se heurte à des difficultés d'équivalence peut se voir obligé à recourir à un outil grammatical jusqu'alors laissé en marge de la langue courante et même à forcer l'emploi de cet outil; d'autre part, une tendance latinisante peut être considérée comme une sorte d'exagération révélatrice d'un état latent.[26]

Thus, Jean de Vignay's predilection for absolute participial constructions is doubtless conditioned by the ablative absolute in the corresponding Latin, but there is nothing syntactically aberrant about his usage (32): 'Et la maison ainssi embrasee, mon compaignon issi hors avec le vallet'. The absolute construction of the Latin has been repeated in the French: 'Ipsa (domo *added BC*; autem *added C*) sic accesa (*l.* accensa?), socius meus cum famulo exivit domum'. It is perhaps noteworthy that *L* has avoided the construction, by adding a conjunction: 'Et quant la maison fu ainsi embrasee'. Then as now, this construction (cf. also 31) was perfectly admissible in French. A similar case arises with the concessive *soit posé que*: in a phrase such as 'Soit posé que le pere d'aucun soit malade' (34), the influence of the Latin concessive construction 'ponatur enim quod . . .' is very clear, even if *(soit) posé que* is attested independently of translations (cf. also 35, 'posé soit . . .'). When Jean de Vignay writes (30) 'Quar en tout le monde n'est autre foy que ceste, qui puisse .i. homme faire sauf', we can probably deduce that the Latin text, 'Nam ab hac (ab hac *omitted C*) non est in mundo (Nam . . . mundo *omitted B*) fides (fides *omitted C*) aliqua que salvum faciat nisi ista', has influenced him, although the construction with *faire* + accusative + adjective was of course perfectly feasible in Middle French. It is, again, noticeable that *L* provides a freer version: '. . . par quoi .i. home puist estre sauvé'. The translation of the Latin conjunction *ut* as *que* (33) seems to come into the same category of influence rather than real calque: manuscript *P* has 'nous montames en une autre nef qui est nommee "coque", [. . .], que nous alissons en Ynde La Haute' where the Latin text reads '. . . ut in Indiam superiorem nos irremus'. Here, too, *L* seems to have produced what is arguably a more natural rendering: 'pour aler en Ynde La Haute', and this may suggest some disquiet about transposing the Latin directly into French. The copyist of *L* displays some reluctance to adopt the apparent calques of Latin verb tenses which *P* exhibits: thus, *P* offers (26) 'tantost l'air est fait si luisant et si cler que touz s'en mer-veilloient' as a version of 'statim aer clarus et lucidus est effectus', but *L* has 'fu fait'. *Fui miratus* produces, in *P*, 'fui je merveillié', where *L* uses an alternative, and perhaps more familiar, verb, 'fu je moult esbahi' (28). To translate the causal conjunction *cum, P* has (25) 'comme tele loy soit felonnesse et plaine de pestilence et fausse et est toute contre Dieu et contre le salu des ames' for the Latin 'cum ipsa sit pestifera et falsa, tamquam contra deum et animarum salutem'. This use of *comme* + subjunctive is not necessarily a Latinism,[27] but it is sufficiently uncommon for it to be likely that the Latin mood has influenced the translator in this case. *L*, at any rate, sidesteps the problem: 'quer tele loy est felonnesse'.

Finally, where the Latin text reads (36) '. . . quam dicunt gentes esse lacrimas quas Adam et Eve effuderunt. Quod tamen non creditur esse verum', both manuscripts avoid the accusative and infinitive in the first clause, but *P* slavishly follows the passive construction in the second, producing 'et dient la gent que ce sont les pleurs et les lermes que Eve et Adam plorerent, laquel chose toutevoies si n'est pas creue estre vraie', whereas *L* has the less clumsy 'toutefoiz n'est pas a croire' for this last clause.

This brings us to the two major areas in which Jean de Vignay's syntax is at its most Latinate, and its least French. These are when confronted with the (frequent) accusative-and-infinitive constructions in the original Latin and, what is perhaps most likely to *dérouter le lecteur*, whether modern or, I suspect, medieval, his handling of the passive verb *videor*, 'to seem'. Infinitive constructions in Middle French expanded to include the so-called 'proposition infinitive savante', a direct object plus infinitive — in 90 per cent of cases, *estre* — after verbs of thinking, saying, hoping, or ordering. It has been suggested, by Charles Brucker,[28] that this is not, strictly speaking, or at any rate not exclusively, a learned form, since it is found in texts where there is no discernible Latin influence; in the case of a translation, however, it is legitimate to conclude that there is surely *some* contamination from the Latin. As Brucker himself puts it,

le traducteur valorise des tendances latinisantes qui, souvent, existaient déjà, à l'état latent, dans la langue.[29]

It would be misleading to suggest that Jean de Vignay is always influenced by this syntactic form: we have just seen that he is perfectly capable of translating it freely, and indeed normally does so without recourse to the French equivalent (cf. 40–6). Thus, in a typical case (41), he writes 'Quar nous voion bien que vous estes bons et sains, et que vostre foi est bonne et vraie et sainte', where the original reads 'nam (bene *added BCY*) videmus vos esse bonos homines (homines *omitted CY*) et sanctos et fidem vestram esse veram sanctam et bonam'. Two accusative-and-infinitive constructions are thereby eschewed. Sometimes, *L* avoids the construction where *P* succumbs: where the Latin text reads: 'ille Fr. Thomas Christum esse verum Deum et hominem probavit rationibus et exemplis', *P* translates as 'celui Frere Thomas leur prouva par raisons et par examples celui estre vrai Dieu et homme', but *L* has '. . . que il estoit vrai Dieu et vrai home' (38). Or (an isolated case, 37) a mistake in one manuscript may highlight the construction: 'Et si comme icels desloiaus disputassent avec ces freres, il disoient Jhesu Crist estre seul pur homme et non pas Dieu', translating 'dicebant Christum solum purum hominem esse et non Deum' in manuscript *P*, comes out as '. . . estre seul *pour* homme' in *L*. It is tempting to conclude that this is not simply a scribal error, but reveals some misunderstanding of the construction in French.

As with the accusative-and-infinitive, so with the passive *videor*: it is by no means invariably literally translated. Where the Latin text has 'Et tot et tanta mercimonia in ista civitate sunt quod multis incredibile videretur', for example, the translation reads 'Et en cele cité sont tant et si grans marcheandises, que ce seroit chose non croiable a mout de gens' (54, cf. 55). Syntactic calques (and there is no shortage of them) produce French which ranges from being relatively straightforward to decipher to being almost impenetrable. In the easy category come such sentences as the following (47): 'Et en ceste terre certes a mout bonnes yaues. Et la raison de ceste chose est veue estre ceste: quar les vaines et les sourses de ces yaues sont veues naistre et esboulir du flueve d'Eufrates', translating 'Hec autem habet bonas aquas, cuius ratio esse videtur (*CY*: est hec ut videtur): nam vene harum aquarum oriri videntur et scaturire a flumine Euphrate' (cf. also 49). An intermediate position is occupied by the phrase (48) 'vous qui estes veus estre hommes raisonnables . . .', the apparent equivalent of 'vos qui homines videmini rationabiles'; manuscript *L*'s 'vous qui deussiés estre home resonnables' is harder to explain, and appears wrong, since the sense of the original is clearly 'seem to be rational beings' (the context is Odoric's vain attempt to dissuade the in-habitants of the (so far unidentified) island of Dondin from eating their dead relatives). In all these cases, the calques of the Latin are transparent. There are even examples where the French text contains similar syntactic oddities and where the absence of an obvious equivalent in any of the (published) manuscripts suggests either that the translator has simply become contaminated by a frequent-ly encountered construction or, perhaps, that we may postulate the verb *videor* in the presumed original: thus, where the translation reads (51) 'Cestes choses qui sont veues estre bestes . . .', and the printed Latin MSS have no direct equivalent of this construction, we can nonetheless probably assume that Jean de Vignay's original text contained **videntur* (cf. also 50). It is difficult to believe that he would have arrived at this construction unaided. The *nec plus ultra* of syntactic calques involving this verb is when the original Latin uses it in impersonal constructions; and at this point the French really does become 'moitieit latin moitieit romans'. 'Et combien par aventure que il soit veu impossible a aucuns' (52) remains comprehensible as a rendering of 'Et quamquam istud forte (*BCY add* aliquibus) incredibile videatur', but there is worse (53): 'Et si comme je ai ja dit, je vi tant de cors d'ommes mors illeuc que se aucun ne les eust veus, il fust estre veu aussi comme chose incredible', calqued on the Latin 'quod nisi aliquis illa vidisset quasi sibi incredibile videretur'. MS *L* is less clumsy in its handling of the phrase, substituting 'avoit' for the auxiliary 'eust' in the *se* clause and translating the last clause by 'il seroit aussi comme chose imposible a croire', thereby avoiding both the complex syntax and the Latinate *incredible*.

Jean de Meun, in the prologue to his translation of Boethius's *Consolatio Philosophiae*, comments as follows on his aim:

Ja soit ce que tu entendes bien le latin, mais toutevoies est de moult plus legiers a entendre le françois que le latin. [. . .] Or pri tous ceulz qui cest livre verront, s'il leur semble en aucuns lieux que je me soie trop esloingniés des paroles de l'aucteur ou que je aie mis aucunes fois plus de paroles que li aucteur n'i met ou aucune fois mains, que il le me pardoignent. Car se je eusse espons mot a mot le latin par le françois, li livres en fust trop occurs aus gens lais et li clers, neis moienement letré, ne peussent pas legierement entendre le latin par le françois.[30]

There is a certain irony in this, since Boethius himself, in his translation of Porphyry, inclined to literal translation.[31] Jean de Meun, like Jean de Vignay, translated Vegetius (and Jean de Vignay both knew and exploited his predecessor's work). Claude Buridant[32] has demonstrated that the two translators are poles apart: as we have seen, Jean de Vignay favours adhesion to 'la pure verité de la letré'; Jean de Meun, on the other hand, opts for flexibility and freedom. Yet Jean de Meun's last sentence sheds some light on Jean de Vignay's methods. To have *espons* ('expounded, elucidated'[33]) the Latin word-for-word would have produced a work incomprehensible to the laity and of little help to the (lesser?) clergy for whom (apparently) it was to serve as a crib to the Latin. In a way, of course, it is precisely the word-for-word translation which would seem to us to be the most useful crib. But only those who are 'moienement letré', reasonably Latinate (*litteratus* again), would be able to make sense of a too literal translation. One wonders whether the same comment might not be applied to some of Jean de Vignay's syntax. At times it must surely have been distinctly *occurs*, and particularly so for readers who knew no Latin, for whom, presumably, it was primarily intended. This prompts a final comment, and it is very much a question rather than a conclusion. Jean de Vignay was a popular translator, and his translation of Odoric was by no means his last. He continued to enjoy royal favour for another twenty years, at least, after he had completed this translation. Not all medieval translators adopted his approach: it is not even clear that his was the method favoured by the majority.[34] Is it perhaps possible that it appealed to his patrons precisely because it flattered their knowledge of Latin to be confronted with a text which was *entendible* only with some such knowledge? The risk, of course, in such an exercise — and it is a risk which Jean de Vignay does run — is that the finished product will not be *entendible* at all. It may well be better to be castigated by grammarians than not understood by the people,[35] but I am doubtful that the people would always, in practice, have understood the distinctly mysterious word-order[36] which Jean de Vignay's theory of translation tends to produce. Meaning is always conditioned by form: in this case, at times, it seems to be sacrificed to it.

Notes

* I am very grateful to Dr Lynn Williams of the Department of Spanish, University of Exeter, upon whom my ideas have been inflicted at various stages of their gestation, and from whose linguistic expertise this paper has benefited considerably.
1. *Les Voyages en Asie au XIV*ᵉ *siècle du bienheureux Odoric de Pordenone*, edited by Henri Cordier (Paris, 1891).

2. *Sinica Franciscana*, edited by Anastasius Van den Wyngaert (5 vols, Quaracchi, Florence and Rome, 1929–54), I: *Itinera et relationes fratrum minorum s. XIII et XIV*; see also *Cathay and the Way Thither; being a collection of medieval notices of China*, edited by Henri Cordier and Col. Sir Henry Yule, II: *Odoric of Pordenone* (London, 1913 and reprint by Kraus, Nendeln, Liechtenstein, 1967); Lucio Monaco, 'I volgarizzamenti italiani della relazione di Odorico da Pordenone', *Studi mediolatini e volgari*, 26 (1978–79), 179–226; A.C. Moule, 'A Small Contribution to the Study of the Bibliography of Odoric', *T'Oung Pao*, 20 (1921), 301–22; Antonio Sartori, 'Odoriciana: Vita e memorie', *Il Santo*, 6 (1966), 7–65.

3. On whom see particularly Christine Knowles, 'Jean de Vignay. Un traducteur du XIVe siècle', *Romania*, 75 (1954), 353–83.

4. See *Li Livres Flave Vegece de la chose de chevalerie par Jean de Vignay*, edited by Leena Löfstedt (Helsinki, 1982) and *Les Enseignements de Théodore Paléologue*, edited by Christine Knowles (London, 1983).

5. Ed. Löfstedt, p. 38.

6. L.G. Kelly, *The True Interpreter: A History of Translation Theory and Practice in the West* (Oxford, 1979), pp. 82–3 and (for the quotation) p. 206. The additions to the *explicit* (ed. Löfstedt, p. 122) are discussed in Claude Buridant, 'Jean de Meun et Jean de Vignay, traducteurs de l'*Epitoma rei militaris* de Végèce. Contribution à l'histoire de la traduction au moyen âge', *Etudes de Langue et de littérature françaises offertes à André Lanly* (Nancy, 1980), pp. 51–69 (p. 53).

7. Ed. Löfstedt, p. 5.

8. Buridant, *op. cit.*, p. 57; see also Christine Knowles, 'A 14th century imitator of Jean de Meung: Jean de Vignay's translation of the *De re militari* of Vegetius', *Studies in Philology*, 53 (1956), 452–8.

9. See B. Woledge and H. Clive, *Répertoire des plus anciens textes en prose française* (Geneva, 1964), pp. 25–31. For comments on this *topos* and translators' claims to 'truth', see Paul Chavy, 'Les Premiers Translateurs français', *French Review*, 47 (1974), 557–65 (p. 561).

10. Löfstedt, introduction, p. 5 n. 16 and Buridant, *op. cit.*, p. 54, who notes the same phenomenon in a prologue to the *Histoire de France en français de Charlemagne à Philippe-Auguste* (1220/30).

11. Ed. Knowles, p. 21.

12. Much ink has flowed over the word *litteratus*. See particularly H. Grundmann, '*Litteratus — Illitteratus*', *Archiv für Kulturgeschichte*, 40 (1958), 1–65. The debate is summarised in M.T. Clanchy, *From Memory to Written Record: England 1066–1307* (London, 1979), pp. 175–201.

13. Ed. Knowles, p. 22.

14. *Ibid.*, p. 12.

15. Ed. Van den Wyngaert, p. 495.

16. Knowles, *Romania*, 75, p. 367.

17. *Ibid.*, p. 374.

18. Ed. Van den Wyngaert, p. 439.

19. 'Le mouvement de relatinisation est aussi ancien que les débuts de la langue française' (Jacques Chaurand, *Introduction à l'histoire du vocabulaire français* (Paris, 1977), pp. 37–49 (p. 37)). See also Christiane Marchello-Nizia, *Histoire de la langue française aux XIVe et XVe siècles* (Paris, 1979), p. 357 (citing two studies by G. Gougenheim) on the phenomenon of 'relatinisation' whereby French words adopt the orthography and sense of their Latin equivalents.

20. *Le Psautier de Metz. Texte du XIVe siècle*, edited by François Bonnardot (Paris, 1884), p. 2.

21. G. Di Stefano, *Essais sur le moyen français* (Paris, 1977), II, 57, quoted by Buridant, *op. cit.*, n. 46.

22. Serge Lusignan, *Parler vulgairement. Les Intellectuels et la langue française aux XIIIe et XIVe siècles* (Montréal–Paris, 1986), p. 153.

23. Quoted *ibid.*, p. 73.

24. *Psautier de Metz*, prologue, p. 4.

25. Quoted in Lusignan, *Parler vulgairement*, p. 144.

26. Charles Brucker, 'La valeur du témoignage linguistique des traductions médiévales. Les constructions infinitives en moyen français', *Linguistique et philologie (applications aux textes médiévaux). Actes du Colloque des 29 et 30 avril 1977*, edited by Danielle Buschinger (Paris, 1977), pp. 325–44 (p. 339).

27. Robert Martin and Marc Wilmet, *Syntaxe du moyen français* (vol. II of *Manuel du français du moyen âge*, edited by Yves Lefèvre) (Bordeaux, 1980), §88.

28. Buridant, *op. cit.*

29. Brucker, *op. cit.*, pp. 334–5.
30. Text in Buridant, *op. cit.*, p. 55 and (excerpt) in Lusignan, *Parler vulgairement*, p. 149.
31. See W. Schwarz, 'The Meaning of *Fidus Interpres* in medieval translation', *Journal of Theological Studies*, 45 (1944), 73–8 (pp. 73–4).
32. Buridant, *op. cit.*
33. See *TL*, III, 1239 and *AND*, II, 270a.
34. Lusignan, *Parler vulgairement*, pp. 141–2.
35. 'Melius est reprehendant nos grammatici, quam non intelligant populi', to quote Jerome, *Enarrationes in Psalmos*, CXXXVIII, 20; quoted by Michael Richter, 'Latina lingua — sacra seu vulgaris?', *The Bible and Medieval Culture*, edited by W. Lourdaux and D. Verhelst (Leuven, 1979), pp. 16–34 (p. 25).
36. Jerome, of course, claimed that the Bible, exceptionally, should be translated word-for-word: 'Ego non solum fateor, sed libera uoce profiteor me in interpretatione Graecorum absque scripturis sanctis, ubi et uerborum ordo mysterium est, non uerbum e uerbo, sed sensum exprimere e sensu' (*Epistolae*, 57, 5, 2; quoted by Schwarz, *op. cit.*, p. 75 n. 4).

Appendix: Examples of Latinisms

Abbreviations used

AND = *Anglo-Norman Dictionary*, ed. Louise W. Stone, William Rothwell and T.B.W. Reid (London, 1977–)

Hakluyt = Richard Hakluyt, *The Principal Navigations Voyages Traffiques & Discoveries of the English Nation Made by Sea or Over-Land to the Remote and Farthest Distant Quarters of the Earth at any time within the compasse of these 1600 Yeeres* (12 vols, Glasgow, 1903–5), IV (1904)

Marchello-Nizia = Christiane Marchello-Nizia, *Histoire de la langue française aux XIVe et XVe siècles* (Paris, 1979)

Martin/Wilmet = Robert Martin and Marc Wilmet, *Syntaxe du moyen français* (vol. 2 of the *Manuel du français du moyen âge*, sous la direction de Yves Lefèvre) (Bordeaux, 1980)

TL = A. Tobler and E. Lommatzsch (ed.), *Altfranzösisches Wörterbuch* (Berlin, 1925–)

The Latin text is quoted from Anastasius Van den Wyngaert (ed.), *Sinica Franciscana* (5 vols, Quaracchi, Florence and Rome, 1929–54), I: *Itinera et relationes fratrum minorum s. XIII et XIV* (Quaracchi, 1929); manuscript sigla are those used in this edition.

A. Translation errors

(1) une seule vile (*L*: vielle) chemise (f. 209ʳb)
The Latin text reads '(ferrentes) solum unam (*BY add*: vilem) interulam' (p. 421: Hakluyt (p. 374) and MS British Library, Arundel 13 (related to Hakluyt) have 'camisiam').

(2) un arbre qui est apelé 'faciolus' (f. 210ʳa)
The Latin text, 'In hac contrata quilibet homo ante domum suam habet unum pedem faxiolorum, ita magnum sicut hic esset una columpna. Hic pes faxiolorum, minime dessicatur donec (*BCY*: dummodo) sibi exibeatur aqua' (p. 423) seems to have been misunderstood by Jean de Vignay.

B. Canis Magnus > Le Grant Chien

(3) Et toutevoies le Chien (*L*: Grant Chien) de Tharaie fu mout de foiz en bataille avec cestui roy en champ, lequel Chien il vainqui touzjors et seurmonta (*L*: et il vainqui touzjours et seurmonta celi Grant Chien) (f. 219ʳa–219ʳb)

(4) Toutevoies le Grant Chien, emperiere des Tartariens de Cartage (*L*: Tartage), s'esforça bien d'avoir cele pierre (f. 221ʳb)
The Latin reads: 'magnus Imperator Tartarorum Catay' (p. 453).

(5) Je enquis de ceste Ynde diligaument a crestiens, Sarrazins, ydolatres, et aussi comme touz les officiers du Grant Chien (*L*: Grant Chien que aucuns appellent le Grant Caen) (f. 222ᵛb)

'Du Grant Chien' translates 'magni Canis' (p. 458); the alternative given in *L* does not appear in any printed Latin MS, but is presumably meant to be a phonetic spelling of 'Khan'. It suggests that the copyist (and the author?) was aware of the real meaning of the Latin 'Canis' in this context.

(6) Et il a dedenz cele cité plus de .xij. mille pons, et en chascun pont sont pluseurs gardes, qui gardent cele cité pour le Grant Chien (f. 225ʳa)
'Pro magno Cane' in the Latin (p. 464).

(7) quar chascun feu paie chascun an .i. balis, c'est .i. denier de la terre, a ce (*L*: pour le treu au) Grant Chien (f. 225ʳb)
The only Latin MS to have an equivalent, *B*, reads 'magno Cano' (p. 464, variant (1)).

(8) pour prier que le Grant Chien ait longue vie (f. 225ᵛa)
'Ut roget vitam pro magno Cane' in the Latin text (p. 466).

(9) Et en ceste cité celui emperiere le Grant Chien si a son siege (*L*: Et le Grant Chien, celi emperiere que il nomment le Grant Caen, a son siege) (f. 227ᵛa)
The Latin reads: 'In hac civitate Canis ille magnus suam sedem habet' (p. 472), with no indication of the explanatory gloss provided in *L*.

(10) Et quant le Grant Chien veult vener (f. 227ᵛa)
The Latin text has only 'dominus' here (p. 472).

C. Lexical borrowings and semantic calques

(11) du Marchié Julien (f. 207ʳa)
Literal translation of the Latin 'de Foro Iulii' (p. 413; Friuli, north-west of Trieste). Jean le Long leaves it untranslated: 'Frere Odoric (*or* Odric) de Foro Julii' (see B.N. fr. 12202, f. 108ᵛ; B.N. fr. 2810, f. 97ᵛ; B.N. fr. 1380, f. 95ʳ; Besançon, Bibliothèque Municipale 667, f. 84ᵛ; Berne, Bibliothèque Municipale 125, f. 181ʳ).

(12) ceste cité si est en mi voie d'aler a Thaurisie (f. 207ᵛb)
est via media eundi Tauris (p. 416). Another obvious calque of the Latin text. The normal meaning of 'enmi' is 'within a place, a specific location' (see Marchello-Nizia, pp. 235, 268). For TL, however, (*s.v.* mivoie, VI, 104), it is a substantive.

(13) aussi comme tout le monde respont a cele cité pour marcheandises (*L*: Quer tout le monde vient a cele cité pour toutes marcheandises) (f. 208ʳa)
'Respont a' translates 'correspondet' in the Latin (p. 417): this use of *respondre* is not recorded in the O.F. dictionaries.

(14) Et ceste terre se respont (*L*: contient) du chief de Caldee, jusques outre vers les montaignes (f. 209ʳa). The Latin text reads: 'Hec terra correspondet a capite Caldee versus tramontanam' (p. 420).

(15) quant il sont tenus d'aucune (*L*: ont aucune) enfermeté (f. 215ᵛb)
The Latin reads 'Nam cum ipso morbo aliquo detinentur' (p. 439). The only meaning of *estre tenu de* given in TL is 'verpflichtet (a aucun)' (X, 223).

(16) il font illec .i. signe en la voie ou il font ce qui est dit devant, si que il sachent combien il sont venuz (f. 217ᵛa)
A very literal translation of the Latin: 'signum unum faciunt illic ubi faciunt hoc, ut sciant quantum processerunt' (p. 443). The nearest TL gets to this sense of *combien* is (temporal) 'wie lange' (II, 587); cf. *AND*, I, 127b.

(17) mes toutevoies ont il maisons en (*L*: par) especial (f. 218ᵛa)
Cf. the Latin: 'Domus autem habentur in speciali' (p. 445). TL gives, for *par especial*, 'besonders' (III, 1168); *AND* has 'specifically' (II, 265a).

(18) Et donc je m'aplicai a (*L*: Et de la m'en alai a) une cité qui a .i. pont a travers par desus ce flueve (f. 224ʳb)
Semantic Latinism from 'aplicui' (which is not reflexive, p. 462). This sense is not given in TL (I, 452–3), but is recorded in Anglo-Norman (cf. *AND*, I, 33a).

(19) Et si comme je me departi des terres de cele contree, en venant vers occident, je m'aplicai a (*L*: je m'aplicai a venir a) une contree qui est apelee Milecorde (f. 233ᵛb)
Semantic borrowing, from the Latin 'aplicui ad quandam contratam' (p. 488)?

(20) Et s'il avient que aucuns de ces gens muire qui soit de ce nombre conté (*L*: gens qui est conté en ce nombre muire) (f. 229ʳb)

The Latin reads: 'Et si aliquem istorum mori contigeret qui de numero computatur' (p. 476).

(21) sans les ylles toutevoies qui sont subjectes a l'empire, qui sont bien .v. mille, qui ne sont point mises en nombre (f. 229ᵛa)

'. . . qui etiam in numero non ponuntur' in the Latin text (p. 476).

(22) Et ainssi par ceste maniere en .i. jour naturel (*L*: en .i. jor naturel, c'est assavoir jour et nuit) (f. 229ᵛb)

MS *L* has glossed the expression *jour naturel*, a literal translation of 'in una die naturali' (p. 477). It is attested in Philippe de Thaon (*AND*, IV, 441b, also quoted in TL).

(23) Et si comme je ai ja dit, je vi tant de cors d'ommes mors illeuc que se aucun ne les eust (*L*: avoit) veus, il fust estre veu aussi comme chose incredible (*L*: il seroit aussi comme chose imposible a croire) (f. 235ʳa) *Incredible* is a learned borrowing, and is not found (in the sense of 'unbelievable'), until Deschamps (cf. TL, IV, 1369–70).

(24) si fait crier que il se tiengnent a pais, et que il aient misericorde des bestes qui sont remeses vives que il ont mises hors du bois (f. 230ᵛa)

Misericorde ('misericordiam', p. 479), is also found in numerous texts which are not translations (e.g. *Renart*): see TL, VI, 93.

D. Syntactic borrowing

(25) comme tele loy soit felonnesse (*L*: quer tele loy est felonnesse) et plaine de pestilence et fausse et est toute contre Dieu et contre le salu des ames (f. 211ʳa)

The Latin reads: 'cum ipsa sit pestifera et falsa, tamquam contra Deum et animarum salutem' (p. 427).

(26) Et si comme il orent rendu les ames (*L*: Et quant il orent rendues les ames) a Dieu par leur martyre, tantost l'air est (*L*: fu) fait si luisant et si cler que touz s'en merveilloient (*L*: que tuit se merveilloient) forment (f. 213ʳb)

Calqued, perhaps, on the Latin: 'Dum autem sic ex martirio suo animas Deo dedissent, statim aer clarus et lucidus est effectus' (p. 432).

(27) Toutes les fames qui la sont mariees ont .i. grant baril ou vessel de cor que il portent en leur chief, si que il soient congneues que il soient mariees (*L*: congneues estre mariees) (f. 224ʳb)

Calque on the passive in the Latin: '. . . ut agnoscantur (*BCYV*: cognoscantur) quod nupte sunt' (p. 462)? 'Il' for 'eles' suggests some difficulty.

(28) Et dont fui je merveillié comme (*L*: Et donc fu je moult esbahi comment) tant de cors pooient habitier ensemble (f. 225ʳb)

Syntactic calque on the tense of the Latin deponent verb, 'fui miratus' (p. 465). *Merveill(i)er* can be used intransitively (TL, V, 1549).

(29) ne je ne fui onques osé aprochier a cele forme (*L*: forme ou figure) d'omme (f. 235ʳa–235ʳb).

Estre osé + infinitive seems to be a syntactic Latinism, based on the original 'Ad ipsam autem faciem nunquam fui ausus totaliter appropinquare' (p. 492); recorded only in translations (see TL, VI, 1338: 'n'ient oseiz avant venir' quoted as a translation of 'non ausus accedere' in the *Dialogues de Grégoire*).

(30) Quar en tout le monde n'est autre foy que ceste (*L*: n'est foi ne creance fors ceste), qui puisse .i. homme faire sauf (*L*: par quoi .i. home puist estre sauvé) (f. 211ʳb)

The Latin text, 'Nam ab hac (ab hac *omitted C*) non est in mundo (Nam . . . mundo *omitted B*) fides (fides *omitted C*) aliqua que salvum faciat nisi ista' (p. 428), appears to have influenced the translator, although the construction is of course perfectly feasible (cf. TL, III, 1575).

(31) Et donc ceulz ainssi hardiement responnans et tres fermement, celui crestien qui les avoit acompaigniez et ces autres .iiij. hommes tençoient mout ensemble (f. 213ʳa)

The participial construction seems, here, to owe something to the Latin ablative absolute construction: 'Unde sic (sic autem *B*) illis audacter respondentibus (constantius *added BY*)' (p. 432).

(32) Et la maison ainssi embrasee (*L*: Et quant la maison fu ainsi embrasee), mon compaignon issi hors avec le vallet (*L*: li et le vallet) (f. 214ᵛb)

The Latin absolute construction has been repeated: 'Ipsa (domo *added BC*; autem *added C*) sic accesa (*l.* accensa?), socius meus cum famulo exivit domum' (p. 436).

(33) nous montames en une autre nef qui est nommee 'coque', [. . .], que nous alissons en Ynde (*L*: pour aler en Ynde) La Haute a Çayton (f. 215ᵛa)
The Latin text has '. . . ut in Indiam superiorem nos irremus ad quamdam civitatem Çaitum' (p. 438).

(34) Soit posé que le pere d'aucun soit malade (f. 222ʳa)
Influence of the Latin concessive construction 'ponatur enim quod . . .' (p. 456); *(soit) posé que* is attested independently (cf. TL, VII, 1634).

(35) Ceste coustume et autre est eue (*L*: ont il) en cele contree. Quar posé soit que le pere d'aucun muire (f. 232ᵛb)
Cf. the Latin introductory concessive 'nam ponatur quod . . .' (p. 485).

(36) et dient la gent que ce sont les pleurs et les lermes que Eve et Adam plorerent, laquel chose toutevoies si n'est pas creue estre vraie (*L*: toutefoiz n'est pas a croire) (f. 221ᵛa)
The Latin text reads: '. . . quam dicunt gentes esse lacrimas quas Adam et Eve effuderunt. Quod tamen non creditur esse verum' (p. 454).

E. Accusative-and-infinitive constructions

(37) Et si comme icels desloiaus disputassent avec ces freres il disoient Jhesu Crist estre seul pur (*L*: pour) homme et non pas Dieu (f. 210ᵛa)
The error (in *L*) highlights the construction: the Latin text has 'dicebant Christum solum purum hominem esse et non Deum' (p. 426).

(38) celui Frere Thomas leur prouva par raisons (*L*: par vive raison) et par examples celui estre vrai Dieu et homme (*L*: que il estoit vrai Dieu et vrai home) (f. 210ᵛb)
The Latin text reads: 'ille Fr. Thomas Christum esse verum Deum et hominem probavit rationibus et exemplis . . .' (p. 426).

(39) que je oÿ dire a gens dignes de foy, qui en la commune parole des dites contrees me tesmoignoient les choses que je ne vi mie, estre vraies (f. 236ʳb)
Calque of the Latin, 'Comunis autem locutio illarum contratarum illa que non vidi testatur esse vera' (p. 494).

(40) se le feu nous art il ne vendra pas (*L*: ce ne sera pas) par defaute de nostre foi, mes tant seulement de (*L*: mes sera tant seulement pour) nos pechiez (f. 211ʳb)
The translator has avoided the construction: cf. 'si ignis nos comburet non hoc credas ex fide nostra procedere sed solum ex peccatis nostris' (p. 427).

(41) Quar nous voion bien (*L*: Nous veons bien) que vous estes bons et sains, et que vostre foi est bonne et vraie et sainte (*L*: et que vostre loy est bonne et sainte) (f. 212ʳb)
The translator avoids the accusative and infinitive in the original: 'nam (bene *added BCY*) videmus vos esse bonos homines et sanctos et fidem vestram esse veram sanctam et bonam' (p. 430).

(42) Et quant l'emperiere du païs oï que ces freres orent soustenu tel sentence (f. 214ʳa–214ʳb)
The Latin reads: 'Audiens autem ipse (ipse *omitted BC*) Imperator Dehli istos fratres talem subiisse penam (sententiam *BCY*)' (p. 435); the translator avoids the construction.

(43) Et touz ceulz de cele contree aourent .i. buef pour leur dieu, et dient que c'est .i. saint (*L*: que il est saint) (f. 216ʳb)
The Latin has an accusative and infinitive: 'Omnes in hac contrata adorant bovem pro deo suo, dicentes ipsum esse quid (*Y*: quasi) sanctum' (p. 440).

(44) et se boutent souz ce char, et en font les roes passer par desus els, et dient que il veulent morir pour leur dieu (f. 217ᵛb)
Cf. the Latin: 'et ponunt se sub isto curru, facientes eum per super se transire, cum dicant se velle mori pro Deo suo' (pp. 443–4).

(45) Et eulz se moquoient mout de moi. Car il disoient que Dieu avoit fait Adam tout nu, et je me vouloie vestir maugré sien (f. 218ʳb)
Cf. the Latin: 'Hii de me multum truffabant, quia dicebant Deum (*ABC*: Deus) Adam fecisse hominem nudum, et ego me malo suo velle vestire volebam' (p. 445).

(46) et dient la gent que ce sont les pleurs et les lermes que Eve et Adam plorerent, laquel chose toutevoies si n'est pas creue estre vraie (*L*: toutefoiz n'est pas a croire) (f. 221ᵛ a)
The Latin text reads: '. . . quam dicunt gentes esse lacrimas quas Adam et Eve effuderunt. Quod tamen non creditur esse verum' (p. 454).

F. Use of *videor*

(47) Et en ceste terre certes a mout bonnes yaues. Et la raison de ceste chose est veue estre ceste: quar les vaines et les sourses de ces yaues sont veues naistre et esboulir du flueve d'Eufrates (f. 207ᵛ b)
Latin text: 'Hec autem habet bonas aquas, cuius ratio esse videtur (*CY*: est hec ut videtur): nam vene harum aquarum oriri videntur et scaturire a flumine Euphrate' (p. 416).

(48) Car se .i. chien estoit occis et mis devant .i. autre chien, si n'en mengeroit il en nulle maniere; et vous qui estes veus estre hommes raisonnables (*L*: vous qui deussiés estre home resonnable), si faites si grant bestiauté (f. 222ᵛ a)
The Latin text reads 'nedum (*l.* necdum?) vos qui homines videmini rationabiles' (p. 457).

(49) Et celui qui estoit veu estre (*L*: estre veu) le plus petit ydole estoit bien aussi grant comme seroit saint Christofle (f. 223ᵛ b)
The Latin reads: '. . . et unum illorum ydolorum, qui minus aliis esset videbatur, erat bene ita magnum sicut esset S. Christoforus' (p. 460).

(50) Et toutevoies ceste terre selonc sa pourporcion est veue une des (*L*: est une des) meilleurs qui soit aussi comme el monde (f. 224ʳ a)
MS *P* contains an apparent Latinism not found in any of the (printed) Latin texts: the SF edition reads 'hec terra de melioribus est que hodie sint in mundo' (p. 461).

(51) Cestes choses qui sont veues estre bestes, si sont les ames des nobles homes que nous repaisson ici pour l'amour de dieu (f. 226ʳ a)
The printed Latin MSS have no direct equivalent of this construction: 'Hec animalia sunt anime nobilium virorum, que nos pascimus amore Dei' (p. 467).

(52) Et combien par aventure que il soit veu impossible a aucuns, toutevoies puet il estre ausi voir (f. 232ʳ a)
An involved syntactic calque of the Latin: 'Et quamquam istud forte (*BCY add* aliquibus) incredible videatur, tamen ista possunt (*CY*: ita potest) esse vera (*Y*: verum)'

(53) Et si comme je ai ja dit, je vi tant de cors d'ommes mors illeuc que se aucun ne les eust (*L*: avoit) veus, il fust estre veu aussi comme chose incredible (*L*: il seroit aussi comme chose imposible a croire) (f. 235ʳ a)
The French text (especially in MS *P*) is calqued, infelicitously, on the Latin impersonal construction, 'quod nisi aliquis illa vidisset quasi sibi incredibile videretur' (pp. 491–2).

(54) Et en cele cité sont tant et si grans marcheandises, que ce seroit chose non croiable a mout de gens (f. 216ʳ b)
The translator has avoided the potential calque in the Latin, 'Et tot et tanta mercimonia in ista civitate sunt quod multis incredibile videretur' (p. 440).

(55) Et aussi y a il mout d'autres choses qui seroient par aventure non croiables a aucuns s'il ne les veoient, pour quoi je n'ai cure d'escrire les (f. 220ᵛ b)
The translator has avoided following the original, which is 'Sic etiam de multis aliis que forte aliquibus incredibilia viderentur nisi illa viderent' (pp. 451–2), too closely.

Prosimetrum in *Le Livre dit Grace Entiere sur le fait du gouvernement d'un Prince*, the Governance of a Prince treatise in British Library MS Royal 16 F ii

Timothy Hobbs

I am delighted to be able to give public expression to the personal debt of gratitude which I owe to John Fox for all his help, interest and encouragement over the years. Christine de Pisan wrote the following lines in her *Livre du chemin de longue estude*:

> Moult m'avez fait grant courtoisie,
> Qui a longue estude mené
> M'avez, car je suis destiné
> A y user toute ma vie[1]

and I am sure that that is a sentiment which will be echoed by all of John Fox's former students, whether or not they have been able to be here this week.

The picture illustrated in Plate 1 is probably one of the best known of medieval manuscript miniatures. It appears, amongst many other places, in John Fox's 1969 book on the lyric poetry of Charles d'Orléans,[2] and shows the poet, captive in the Tower of London, sitting writing at a table, whilst on another side he is seen again, looking out of a window. Below, outside the White Tower, he is seen a third time, giving a messenger a letter for the Duke of Burgundy, no doubt with a copy of the poem which the illumination accompanies, in which he asks for help in raising his ransom.[3] The miniature is taken from the British Library manuscript Royal 16 F ii, a beautiful volume compiled in 1500 for Prince Arthur, Prince of Wales. The manuscript contains the poems which Charles wrote up to the time of his release from captivity in 1440, but in an order which differs significantly from that of the autograph manuscript in the Bibliothèque Nationale, which formed the basis of Pierre Champion's edition of the poems.[4] The significance of the order of the poems in Royal 16 F ii was lucidly and convincingly explained when 44 of them were edited by John Fox in 1973, in the Exeter French Texts series.[5] In that edition, for a Frontispiece, Professor Fox chose not to reproduce

Plate 1. *Charles d'Orléans in the Tower of London: MS Royal 16 F ii, f.73.*
(By permission of the British Library)

once more the picture of Charles d'Orléans in the Tower, but decided instead to draw attention to the identity of the manuscript's dedicatee by reproducing the miniature on f.210 verso of the manuscript, which shows a prince surrounded by his advisers. This is the illumination which accompanies the fourth and final text in the manuscript, a treatise in verse and prose in which a prince is taught the art of good and wise government. The author tells his princely reader that if he rules wisely and judiciously, following the precepts given in this work, he will earn the love of his subjects, and this in turn will enable him, 'après sa seigneurie mondaine', to achieve complete grace in the eyes of God. It is from this phrase that the text derives its title, *Le Livre dit Grace Entiere sur le fait du gouvernement d'un prince*, and it is with this as yet virtually unknown text that this paper is concerned.

The text of *Grace entiere*, at least in Royal 16 F ii, consists of a verse introduction of 158 lines, a main section in prose, occupying 30 folios of the manuscript, and a concluding section of 178 lines of verse.[6] What I should like to do in this paper is to spend some time outlining the background of the *Grace entiere* text as it is found in the British Library manuscript, and then, by way of a brief *coda*, to examine the relationships between the outer verse sections and the main section in prose, and to explore the relationship between the text's didactic purpose and the prosimetrical form in which it is written.

Manuscript Royal 16 F ii is a volume of 248 folios of beautifully written text, accompanied by some excellent border illumination and line fillers in the Flemish style, and by six full-page miniatures, which again are of very high quality. Three of these, including the famous Tower of London illumination (Plate 1), illustrate the collection of poems by Charles d'Orléans which occupies just over half of the volume. The fourth miniature occurs at the beginning of the manuscript's second text, *Les Epistres de l'Abesse Heloys*, in which Heloys gives conventional advice on matters of love to her young disciple Gaultier, from the 'Abbaye du Paraclit' to which she has retired. The third text of the manuscript is called *Les Demandes d'Amour*, and consists of 105 questions and answers on the theme of love. As in the *Epistres de l'Abesse Heloys*, the tone is didactic, and the views expressed are entirely conventional.

The manuscript's final illumination is that which illustrates *Grace entiere* (Plate 2). It uses the same iconographic technique of 'continuous representation' as the miniature of Charles d'Orléans in the Tower, and shows the prince standing under a dais on the left, magnificently dressed and wearing a crown of fleurs de lys. He is reading a paper (possibly the text of *Grace entiere* itself) in the presence of six of his advisers, including two priests. On the right, in the foreground a greyhound lies expectantly, whilst in the background the prince is seen again in an even more splendid cloak, kneeling before an altar where a priest is celebrating Mass.

Throughout the manuscript, the borders of the illuminations are as fine as the

Plate 2. *The prince surrounded by his counsellors: MS Royal 16 F ii, f.210v.*
(By permission of the British Library)

miniatures themselves. Recurring images in the borders include greyhounds, dragons, lions, red Lancaster roses, white York roses, and roses symbolically quartered with red and white. The portcullis, symbol of the Tudors, and ostrich feathers, symbol of the Prince of Wales, with his motto 'Ic dene', are frequently represented, and almost all the borders include typically Flemish representations of foliage and flowers, birds, butterflies and fruits.

These iconographic details, coupled with internal evidence in the texts themselves, have led scholars to conclude that the manuscript was compiled in 1500 for the then Prince of Wales, Arthur, the elder son of Henry VII. One or two French scholars, including Champion in his edition of Charles d'Orléans's poems,[7] have maintained that the manuscript was composed for Arthur's younger brother Henry, later Henry VIII; but this attribution is clearly mistaken. The error is corrected by John Fox in the introduction to his Exeter French Texts edition of the Charles d'Orléans poems,[8] where he convincingly argues that the special order of the poems in Royal 16 F ii, and the nature of the other texts in the manuscript, confirm that the manuscript was compiled with Arthur in mind, at a time when the fourteen-year-old prince was still awaiting the arrival in England of his young bride, Catherine of Aragon. Their marriage had been arranged as early as 1489, as a symbol both of the growing strength and public recognition of the newly-established Tudor dynasty of Henry VII, and of the alliance of England under Henry VII with Spain under Catherine's parents, Ferdinand of Aragon and Isabelle of Castile. It was not until 1501, though, that Catherine came to England to meet Arthur; and their marriage took place, with all the pageantry and magnificence that Henry VII could muster, in St Paul's Cathedral in November of that year. Almost immediately after the ceremony, the young couple set off for the Welsh Marches, where Arthur was to resume his role as Prince of Wales. They took up residence at Ludlow Castle where, as Henry's representatives, they received the homage of the Marcher Lords; but their life together was cut tragically short when, on the 2nd April 1502, barely five months after their marriage, Arthur died at the age of only fifteen. The cause of his death is not clear, but it seems to have been either some sort of tubercular illness, or a particularly virulent strain of influenza which we know swept through Ludlow in March 1502. Arthur had never been robust, and he would not have been able to resist for long an epidemic of this sort. Whatever the precise cause of death, Arthur's body lay in state at Ludlow until Saint George's Day, on which symbolic date the young prince, this new Arthur on whom the hopes of the Tudors had depended, and whom Henry had named after that other King Arthur from whom the Tudors claimed descent, was taken to Worcester Cathedral for burial. After his death, the title of Prince of Wales passed to his ten-year-old brother Henry, and it was he, of course, who ascended the throne as Henry VIII after the death of his father in 1509. One of his first acts after his accession was to marry Catherine of Aragon, as his father had arranged should happen after the death of Arthur; but that is another story.

This, then, was the young prince for whom MS Royal 16 F ii was compiled in 1500. The identity of the person responsible for the manuscript's compilation is not given anywhere, but it has been generally agreed for many years[9] that he can be identified as Bernard André, the blind French poet and Augustinian monk, who was employed from about 1496 to about 1500 as Prince Arthur's tutor. Born in Toulouse around 1450, Bernard André had been presented to the future Henry VII during the latter's exile in France. We do not know whether he was present at Bosworth Field in 1485 when Henry defeated Richard III, but we do know that he recited a commemorative poem of praise when Henry entered London in triumph to claim the throne. Later that same year he received a benefice from the king, and from 1486 onwards an annual gift of ten marks. He received a further gift every New Year's Day, possibly as payment for his work as Poet Laureate, a title which he had already acquired by the end of 1486; and he continued to accumulate benefices, which he almost certainly held *in absentia*, under both Henry VII and Henry VIII. The last time his name appears in official records is in 1521, by which time he would have been around 70 years old. Bale, in his *Scriptorum illustrium maioris Britannie* of 1557, says that he died in London, and was buried in the church of the Augustinians there; but of that we have no other proof.[10]

There is nothing in the records of Bernard André's life, or in his surviving works as an author, to confirm or refute the assertion by successive scholars that he was the compiler of Royal 16 F ii. His post as tutor to Prince Arthur certainly makes it possible; but he was not by any means the only Frenchman in Henry VII's court, and, although undoubtedly one of the leading figures in the circle of French and Italian humanists with which Henry VII surrounded himself, he was by no means the only one who would have been capable of bringing together the four texts of Royal 16 F ii into a single volume for presentation to the young prince. For the moment, I am prepared to accept Bernard as the most likely compiler, but I am increasingly unsure about the attribution, and more work needs to be done on the question before it can be accepted without reservation.

The identity of the author of the *Grace entiere* text is as shrouded in uncertainty as that of the compiler of the manuscript as a whole, and here I am afraid I have to disagree with John Fox. In the introduction to his edition of the Charles d'Orléans poems from our manuscript, he says:

Il nous semble fort possible, enfin, que les ouvrages didactiques qui suivent les poésies du duc puissent être attribués à Bernard André, qui a donné ailleurs le témoignage de son talent pour combiner didacticisme et louange de la famille royale anglaise qu'il servait en tant que précepteur, poète et historiographe.[11]

This attribution of the authorship of *Grace entiere* to Bernard André is seductively neat. If it were correct, it would mean that the whole of Royal 16 F ii would become the work of just two people: that is, Charles d'Orléans, whose poems take up the first half of the volume; and Bernard André, who would be responsible both for writing the three remaining texts and for bringing the texts together and arranging them in a way which would particularly suit the young prince whom he had under his tutelage. If the hypothesis were correct, it would mean that we knew when the manuscript was written and compiled, by whom and for whom.

Unfortunately, at least as far as the authorship of *Grace entiere* is concerned, the hypothesis has to be rejected. Not only does our text employ none of the heavily Latinate language and abundant classical imagery which characterise Bernard's other surviving works in French, but also (and far more conclusively) I have been able to locate three English versions of the central prose section of *Grace entiere* which predate the text in the British Library manuscript by some 50 years; and I have also found references to another copy of the complete text in French which antedates our manuscript by more than 125 years. The story of the discovery of these earlier versions of our text makes one of those codicological detective stories which continue to make manuscript studies so exciting and fascinating; but there is not room here for any more than the bare conclusions.[12]

The oldest of these ancestors of our text is a manuscript which belonged from at least 1373 to the magnificent library which Charles V of France kept in the tower of his palace in the Louvre, and which then passed intact to his son, the unfortunate Charles VI, and then to John Duke of Bedford, Regent of France and brother of Henry V of England. The fate of the collection, and of the *Grace entiere* manuscript in particular, after Bedford acquired it in 1425 is unknown. It seems likely that Bedford kept it in France with him for a time, and then it is thought that he had it sent back to England. Wherever it was kept, it is almost certain that the collection was kept intact until Bedford's death in 1435. After that, large numbers of the books were sold, given away as presents, or even borrowed from the library and not returned. Some of the books listed in the inventories reappeared later, and were either bought back by the French, or found their way into other collections in England. But the proportion of books that have been traced in this way is all too small and, alas, the one called *Grace entiere* is not among them. Like all self-respecting originals in the field of manuscript studies, this one is now lost.

Nevertheless, I am as certain as I can be, in the absence of the book itself, that the text in the library of Charles V, Charles VI, and John Duke of Bedford, was the same as we have in Royal 16 F ii; and I am certain moreover that it was in the same verse-prose-verse form as our text. Evidence for this assertion lies in the fact that the missing text and ours have the same distinctive title, which I have not come across anywhere else in the Governance of Princes genre. Even more conclusive is the fact that in the catalogue which was drawn up at Bedford's request in 1423, the entry for the missing manuscript gives the opening words of the second and final folios, and that these same words can be found in corresponding places in our text.[13] Significantly, these are in the text's verse introduction and conclusion; and I take this as fairly conclusive evidence that the *Grace entiere* text in the Charles V library, first listed in the catalogue of 1373, was virtually identical to the text in Royal 16 F ii, made in 1500, and, moreover, that it shared that text's prosimetrical form.

If this conclusion is accepted, then obviously we do not need to look around the court of Henry VII, at Bernard André or anyone else, to find *Grace entiere*'s author. But where do we need to look? It is possible, of course, that the manuscript in Charles V's library was written well before the collection was first catalogued in 1373. It is also possible that the manuscript in Charles V's library was not the original, but was copied from an earlier manuscript, now also lost. Either of these possibilities would push the date of the text's original composition back beyond the 1370s, though we do have a *terminus post quem* in the fact that *Grace entiere* refers on two occasions to the *Livre du Gouvernement des Rois* of Aegidius Romanus, which was written sometime before 1286. Otherwise the original date of composition of *Grace entiere*, and the identity of its author, remain unknown, at least for the time being.

As I said, though, this missing manuscript is not the only copy of *Grace entiere* which predates Royal 16 F ii. I have also located three manuscripts which contain its central prose section in an English translation, and which provide codicological evidence which is crucial both to our understanding of the way in which the text of *Grace entiere* was transmitted, and to discussion of the relationship between the work's verse and prose sections.

All three English manuscripts are roughly contemporaneous, dating from around 1450: they now belong to the collections of the University Library at Harvard, of my own library at Trinity College Cambridge, and of University College Oxford.[14] The first of them has been owned by the University of Harvard since 1878. It is a volume of works by John Lydgate, and *Grace entiere* is included because it was transposed to its present position from another manuscript along with the fifth text of the Harvard volume, Lydgate's *Serpent of Division*.

The manuscript at Trinity is, sadly, the least complete of the three, having lost from the beginning of the text a complete folio (equivalent to five folios of Royal 16 F ii) at some, I think fairly early, point in its history. It is now the third and final text of a volume which was included in the large collection of manuscripts left to Trinity in 1738 by the antiquarian Roger Gale; but, to judge from signs of water damage on the first surviving leaf of the *Grace entiere* text, I suspect that it might once have been the first text in the manuscript.

It is the manuscript belonging to University College Oxford, however, which is in many ways the most interesting of the three, as it could provide important clues to the relationship between the lost original and the other manuscripts in English. It is a handsomely illuminated volume which contains English translations of Alain Chartier's *Quadrilogue invectif* and of the *Secreta secretorum* as well as *Grace entiere*; and there is sufficient internal evidence, in this and other manuscripts composed by the same scribe and illuminator, to lead me to suggest that the link between the missing original of *Grace entiere* and the three mid-fifteenth century English translations of the work is to be found in the person of Sir John Fastolf. Fastolf was not only a great English landowner and a celebrated warrior, who was awarded the Order of the Garter in 1426 for his valorous deeds in France: he was also the Grand Master of the Household of John Duke of Bedford, and one of Bedford's executors after the latter's death in 1435. He was, moreover, a keen bibliophile, and we know that he commissioned English translations of French works from, amongst others, his secretary and stepson, Stephen Scrope. It is my contention that Fastolf might have seen the French original of *Grace entiere* when it was in the possession of the Regent, John Duke of Bedford, and that he had the prose section of it translated into English (possibly, though not necessarily, by Stephen Scrope) either before Bedford's death or after it, at which time Fastolf might even, as executor, have acquired the original for himself. It is clear from internal evidence that none of the three English manuscripts is itself the original translation, but all three are very closely related, and I think it probable that all three were copied from a common source. In the case of the University College manuscript, the work was done by the same scribe and illuminator who also worked on at least one other manuscript for Fastolf, and in the case of the Trinity manuscript, the scribe included another of Scrope's translations in the same manuscript.[15]

This identification of Sir John Fastolf as the central figure around whom revolves the translation of *Grace entiere* into English is based, I admit, on rather circumstantial evidence; but it can be supported in greater detail, and I naturally intend to do so in the published edition of the text. In the meantime, I hope it will be agreed that the theory is at least plausible. If it is the correct hypothesis, then we may even be one step closer to relocating the lost original from the Charles V library.

The interest of these three English translations is obvious. First, the fact that they predate Royal 16 F ii obviously confirms that the British Library text is a copy, not the original, and that our search for the author's identity has to move away from 1500 and Henry VII's court. Second, the fact that the text of the English translations is practically identical to that of the prose section of *Grace entiere* in Royal 16 F ii must mean that the compiler of that manuscript, whether it was Bernard André or someone else, did not attempt to make any significant changes to the prose of the *exemplar* he was copying. If this was so for the prose section, I see no reason to suspect that the verse sections were treated any differently: so we can with some certainty, I think, claim that the verse sections of the Royal 16 F ii text are practically identical to those of the original manuscript. That, it seems to me, further strengthens the case in favour of the lost *Grace entiere* from the Charles V collection being the same as that in Royal 16 F ii: a case, it will be remembered, that is largely based on the matching of the title and of two phrases in the two copies of the text.[16]

There is a third point, which lends further credence to the idea that the lost original was in the same prosimetrical form as the text in Royal 16 F ii. As I have said, the English translations are of just the central prose section of the work; but at three points in the prose, reference is made back to the opening verse section, and these references are included in the English translations even though the verse sections themselves have been omitted. The existence of these cross-references is still further proof, I think, that the original text contained the verse sections; and that in turn strengthens still further the claim of the lost Charles V library text to be the lost original itself.

That, then, is the codicological background to the text in Royal 16 F ii. I should like to finish by considering briefly the work's prosimetrical form, and the relationship between the outer verse sections and the main section in prose. The use of *prosimetrum* is, of course, far from uncommon in medieval French literature; but usually it consists in alternating sections of verse and prose throughout the work in question. I can think of no other example of the particular tripartite form which we find in *Grace entiere*, and this is one reason among many others why I feel that the work deserves to be better known.

In some ways the relationship between the verse and the prose sections is quite simple: the first verse section contains the introduction, in which we are told how the prince made known his desire to own a book to teach him the art of good governance; and the second verse section contains the conclusion, in which the author expresses the hope that the prince will be able to achieve grace in the eyes of God by living according to the precepts contained in the text; while the central prose section contains the main didactic part of the treatise. As far as it goes, this interpretation of the evidence is correct, and it would certainly serve to explain why the verse sections were omitted from the English translations of the text in the manuscripts at Oxford, Cambridge and Harvard: as far as we can tell, these manuscripts were not compiled for, as it were, a practising prince to read, and so the introduction and conclusion were to a large extent irrelevant. However, the evidence is not quite as simple as this interpretation might suggest. As can be seen from the synopsis of the text,[17] the verse sections do not just contain the introduction and the conclusion, but also repeat a good many of the themes that are dealt with in the prose. It is true that the treatment of particular themes is not always absolutely identical in the verse and the prose versions; but the difference is usually very slight, and certainly not significant enough to explain to modern readers why the author felt the need to repeat himself as he does.

I think, in fact, that the correct explanation for the particular prosimetrical structure which we find in *Grace entiere*, with its attendant repetition and occasional prolixity, lies in the medieval mind, and I should like to suggest that the text of *Grace entiere* can be taken as typifying many characteristics of medieval didactic literature, and indeed of medieval thought. For what has the author sought to achieve with his apparently unique prosimetrical construction if not that same tripartite division which was so popular and so pervasive in medieval society? We see it again and again: deriving originally of course from the Trinitarian image of perfection, it is applied, for example, to society as a whole in the traditional divisions of clergy, nobility, and common people; and it is used repeatedly by authors wanting to subdivide their subject matter. The author of *Grace entiere* himself uses the tripartite division when he seeks, albeit not entirely successfully, to divide his advice on good government into three main sections; and the tripartite prosimetrical division of the work's formal structure is a further reflection of the same preoccupation.

Similarly, the way in which the author of *Grace entiere* repeats the same advice in both verse and prose sections would have been entirely familiar to medieval authors and their readers. *Grace entiere* does not of course even remotely approach the literary heights of some other works in its use of internal repetition, but I think it would be fair to say that its underlying aim is the same: to reinforce the message it is seeking to convey, by means of a slightly refocussed restatement of a particular theme or precept. Viewed in this light, the recurrence of the same piece of advice in both the verse and the prose sections of *Grace entiere* is not a weakness but a strength, and the relationship between the different parts of the prosimetrical structure is also strengthened.

It was not just within individual works that medieval authors could be repetitive, of course, and this is especially true of writers of didactic literature, who were quite happy to plagiarise wholesale the work of other authors, frequently without any kind of acknowledgement. Indeed, the genre of the Governance of Princes as a whole was particularly given to this characteristic, whereby certain themes and precepts are copied from one work to another, to such an extent that they become traditional elements of the genre; and in this respect too, *Grace entiere* provides a good example of medieval practice. It is for precisely this reason that the compiler of Royal 16 F ii could turn in 1500 to a text which had been written a century and a quarter earlier, and include it practically unaltered in the manuscript he was putting together for Prince Arthur.

Finally, I think that the modern reader of *Grace entiere* should bear in mind the dictum, given by Horace in his *Ars poetica*, that successful authors mingle profit with pleasure by at the same time delighting and instructing their readers.[18] It was a dictum which was very popular in the Middle Ages, and one to which both the original author of *Grace entiere*, writing sometime before 1373, and the compiler of Royal 16 F ii, working in 1500, would almost certainly have subscribed. It provides a further explanation of the relationship between the work's verse and prose sections. Although the primary aim of the work was didactic, to teach a prince the art of good governance, nevertheless the means by which this aim could be achieved did not preclude the use of octosyllabic couplets and other poetic devices, or indeed of attractive illuminations and miniatures. In this way too, *Grace entiere* can be seen as typifying a characteristic of medieval French literature.

It is obviously impossible, in a short paper such as this, to do more than indicate a few main areas of interest, especially when one is dealing with a text that is virtually unknown. Nevertheless, I hope that it will be seen that the *Grace entiere* of MS Royal 16 F ii is a text which merits further study, not just because of its interesting codicological background, or because of the identity of its princely dedicatee, but also because it represents a particularly interesting example of French medieval didactic literature, in the way it combines some fairly traditional themes with an apparently unique formal structure.

Appendix: Synopsis of *Grace entiere* in British Library MS Royal 16 F ii

The verse introduction starts with a short prologue: in the year 1500, a young prince announces that he would like to own a book in which he can learn the art of good government. He is overheard by some of his advisers, who obtain for him a copy of the work called *Grace entiere*. The treatise itself starts with the organic analogy found in so many Governances of Princes: the prince's country is compared to the human body, of which the prince himself is the head. This analogy is followed by the first piece of advice on good government, namely that the prince should know himself in order to understand others. It is at this point, after 75 lines on this subject, that the verse section abruptly stops, and the author continues in prose, saying by way of a reason that he realises that teaching and instruction can often bore the reader

> Quant ilz sont trop longs et prolis   151 (f.214r)
> Ou de langaige trop polis,
> Pource vueil je laisser la rime
> Et le langaige leonime
> Pour parler en briefve maniere
> Et par poursieute plus legiere
> Ce dont j'ay dit aucune chose,
> Sique j'en parleray en prose.

After briefly mentioning some of the work's principal sources, the prose section resumes the advice that had already been started at the end of the verse, that the prince should know himself in order to govern others with humility and charity.

This is then followed by the work's second main section, which contains advice on how the prince should dispose of his rents and revenues, and which is itself divided into three subsections: such revenues should be used for the necessary expenses of his household; for works of charity 'par lesquelles l'en acquiert l'amour de Dieu et sauvement de l'ame', rewards for good service, and necessary buildings such as fortresses; and for building up the country's reserves.

In the third section, which is said to be 'le principal en l'estat du prince pour bien gouverner sa principaulté', the prince is urged to rule justly and unselfishly, with due regard for the fact that he himself will be called to account on the Day of Judgement. This third main section is also subdivided, this time into four, as the author discusses the four virtues of science, foresight, justice, and mercy, by which the prince will be able to rule justly. This is then followed by shorter sections on the prince's choice of advisers and officers; on the duties and obligations which the prince and his family have towards each other; and on the conduct which the prince should adopt in time of war.

At this point the text reverts once more to verse, and the remaining 185 lines are largely taken up with a résumé of some of the main ideas which have been discussed in the prose section. Finally, the author brings the work to a close with the prayer that the prince for whom the book has been made might enjoy a long and peaceful reign, secure in the love of his people,

> Syqu'il puisse envers Dieu conquerre   1367 (f.248v)
> Grace entiere, gloire souveraine,
> Aprés sa seigneurie mondaine.

Notes

1. Christine de Pisan, *Le Livre du chemin de long estude*, ed. Robert Püschel (Berlin, 1887; repr. Geneva, 1974), lines 1160–3.
2. John Fox, *The Lyric Poetry of Charles d'Orléans* (Oxford, 1969).
3. In fact, by October 1440, when Charles wrote the poem 'Des nouvelles d'Albion', which the miniature accompanies in Royal 16 F ii, he was no longer being held in the Tower of London, but at Stourton in Wiltshire. See Enid McLeod, *Charles of Orleans, Prince and Poet* (London, 1969), pp. 234–5.
4. Charles d'Orléans, *Poésies*, ed. P. Champion, 2 vols (Paris, 1923–4; repr. 1956).
5. Charles d'Orléans, *Choix de poésies*, ed. John Fox (Exeter, 1973).
6. A brief synopsis of the work's principal points is given as an Appendix to this paper: see pp. 60–61 above.
7. *Op. cit.*, vol. 1, p. xi.
8. *Op. cit.*, pp. xix–xxi.
9. The attribution seems to have been first suggested by G.F. Warner in his *Illuminated Manuscripts in the British Museum* (London, 1903), and to have been accepted by all subsequent scholars, including Pierre Champion and John Fox.
10. For a more detailed description of Bernard André's life, see my unpublished MA dissertation, *Le Livre dit Grace Entiere sur le fait du gouvernement d'un prince: édition critique d'après le MS Royal 16 F ii du British Museum* (University of Exeter, 1975), pp. 49–55.
11. *Op. cit.*, p. xxi.
12. Fuller details will be given in my forthcoming edition of *Grace entiere*. See also the introduction to my unpublished MA dissertation.
13. The manuscript in question, entitled *La Doctrine des Princes nommée Grâce entière*, appears in the catalogue of Charles V's library which Gilles Malet, the royal librarian, drew up in 1373. Further catalogues were drawn up in 1411 and 1413, in both of which *Grace entiere* appears. When Charles VI died in 1422, the attention of John Duke of Bedford was drawn to the existence of this splendid library, and it was on his orders that another inventory of the books in the collection was drawn

up in 1423, as a result of which Bedford decided to buy the entire collection. This last catalogue has been edited by L. Douët d'Arcq in *Inventaire de la Bibliothèque du Roy Charles VI* (Paris, 1867), and at the shelf-mark 64 the following entry appears:

> Item. *La Doctrine des Princes nommée Grâce entière*; couverte
> de soye jaune à deux petiz fermouers d'argent, escripte en françois,
> de lettre formée. Commençant au iie feuillet 'et aucuns', et ou derrenier
> 'faisons par dévote'.

The incipit of the second folio can hardly provide conclusive evidence of a text's identity, even though the same words do appear in the Royal 16 F ii text, at line 41. This is the tenth line of the third page, which would, of course, have been the tenth line of the second folio if the text had started on a recto, not on a verso as it does. The prince has told his counsellors that he would like to have a book in which he could learn the art of good government. The counsellors are delighted;

> Et aucuns de ceulx qui ce ouyrent   41 (f.211v)
> Apres ce diligence firent
> Tant que par eulx est pourveu,
> Et le plustost qu'ilz ont peu,
> Ung livre sur ceste matiere,
> Que l'en appelle *Grace Entiere*.

But 'faisons par dévote', cited in the 1423 catalogue as the opening words of the last folio of the lost manuscript, is much more distinctive; and the last page of Royal 16 F ii, eighteen lines from the end of the text, begins like this:

> A la fin de nostre matiere,   1352 (f.248v)
> De ce livre dit *Grace Entiere*,
> Faisons par devote maniere
> Au Roy des roys nostre pryere,
> Que le prince pour qui ce livre
> Est fait puisse regner et vivre
> Longuement en estat de grace . . .

14. Harvard University Library, MS Eng. 530; Trinity College Cambridge, MS O.5.6; University College Oxford, MS 85.
15. Otto Pächt and J.J.G. Alexander, in *Illuminated Manuscripts in the Bodleian Library Oxford*, 3 vols (Oxford, 1966–73), vol. 1, pp. 54–5, have identified Bodleian Library Oxford, MS Laud Misc. 570 as being possibly the work of the same scribe and illuminator as the University College manuscript. The text in the Trinity manuscript which is known to have been translated by Scrope is *The Dictes and Sayings of the Philosophers*, which occupies ff. 38–67v of the manuscript.
16. See note 13 above. The only lines of the verse sections which have obviously been altered by the compiler of Royal 16 F ii are the opening two lines of the whole work, where the date 1500 is given, albeit in an extraordinarily convoluted way.
17. See the Appendix, pp. 60–61 above.
18. Horace, *Ars poetica*, lines 343–4:

> Omne tulit punctum qui miscuit utile dulci,
> Lectorem delectando pariterque monendo

(He has gained every vote who has mingled profit with pleasure by both delighting the reader and instructing him.)

Form and Meaning in *Aucassin et Nicolette*

Roger Pensom

This is a text that has given rise to a fair amount of critical anxiety. The story is much loved and has been much read, but largely because of the problems associated with its remarkable narrative structure, criticism of the text in recent years has taken a distinctly positivistic turn. The problem of locating its affective impact in its structure has generally proved too much and the mechanisms of displacement have operated, deflecting critical attention to the historical questions associated with the text. Howard Bloch, the neo-positivist wolf posing as post-structuralist lamb, denies this text the attribute of literarity, seeing in the episode of Torelore the collapse of intelligibility as a necessary consequence of the gainsaying of reproductive processes in the biological sense.[1] Tony Hunt has called for a return to the classification of folktale motifs in the story as an antidote to woolly speculation on its status as parody.[2] Kevin Brownlee, another neo-positivist flying narratological colours, sees Nicolete as the 'disguise adopted by the author figure for himself in his own text.'[3] A conspiracy is afoot for the collective denial of the story's status as poetic structure. It seems on the face of it incredible that this body of influential critical writing should, in an age much concerned with the semiological function of language, be so unconcerned by the structure and meaning of its collective strategy of displacement. This is not to say that history and taxonomy are not important and interesting; it's just to say that poetry is too. Historical scholarship overreaches itself when it marginalises the semiological properties of the fictional text, ignoring the fact that the metaphorical/connotational and the metonymic/denotational are interdependent functions of natural language, a degree-zero of either being unimaginable. For example, Bloch's absolutisation of the metonymic/denotational function abolishes the 'poetic' function of the text (Jakobson's terminology), and gives rise to a discourse from which stylistic description is excluded. This privileging of the metonymic/linear function of narrative at the expense of the metaphorical/intensive mode, is a game that is still being played, a game that pre-supposes the validity of the classic Comtian league table in which prose supersedes poetry and science replaces magic and religion.

I would like to return to an earlier insight of Leo Spitzer. In an article of 1950 he writes as follows:

C'est cette idée du développement intérieur indépendant des 'enfans' vers la maturité

63

d'époux heureux qui forme l'unité des différents épisodes du chantefable qu'on a discutés séparément (sous l'obsession de la recherche des sources).[4]

Here Spitzer pinpoints a persistent feature of positivist criticism, the vision of the text as an aggregate, rather than as a system. Rogger describes the story as 'une mosaïque de réminiscences littéraires',[5] but this is only true insofar as the narrative syntax redefines the semantic value of each constitutive element functionally in terms of its relations with other elements. Spitzer's remark implies a structural rather than a taxonomic approach to the text as well as privileging its affective and human value as an intentional[6] structure. I would like to take another look at the text from his point of view, to try and say something intelligible about the way our feelings about the text relate to the patterns of its organisation.

The text opens with the confrontation between parents and son. Aucassin refuses to fight his father's enemy because his father will not let him marry the girl he loves.[7] Mother too adheres to the patrilineal principle. Nicolete is imprisoned to keep her out of the way. These events inaugurate the central theme of the text, which, I suggest, is the social repression of the symbolic feminine and the eventual return of the repressed in the anagnorisis of the final union of the lovers. The problem of sexual identity in its relation to social structure is raised during the development of this theme and the text has some very interesting things to say about it. It points, for example, to the plasticity of sexual identity as a symbolic function of the subject. In the first verse interlude, Aucassin's mother, identifying herself with the paternal role, reprimands him for his betrayal of genealogy:

> Di va! faus, que vex tu faire?
> . . .
> Puis qu'a moullier te vix traire
> Pren femme de haut parage.'   (p. 3)

The descriptions of the lovers, which involve a literal repetition, designate through that repetition a single undifferentiated space into which social and sexual difference will be written:

(Aucassin) il avoit les caviax blons et menus recercelés et les ex vairs et rians et le face clere et traitice et le nes haut et bien assis. Et si estoit enteciés de bones teces qu'en lui n'en avoit nule mauvaise se bone non. (2)
(Nicolete) Ele avoit les caviaus blons et menus recercelés et les ex vairs et rians, et le face traitice, et le nes haut et bien assis, e les levretes vremelletes plus que n'est cerise ne rose. (14)

Here we are told that the text sees sexual difference as a symbolic variable, rather than something written into Nature. (I shall leave the general question of the semiological function of repetition in this text for another time.) As a psychological attribute its value fluctuates, as we see in the battle scene, between the parameters of activity/passivity and Pleasure/Reality.[8] Aucassin's father Garin has promised Nicolete to his son as a reward for defeating his enemy, the Count of Valens. As Aucassin goes into battle, we read:

Or ne quidiés vous qu'il pensast n'a bués n'a vaces n'a civres prendre, ne qu'il ferist cevalier ne autre lui. Nenil nient! onques ne l'en sovint; ains pensa tant a Nicolete sa douce amie qu'il oublia ses resnes et quanque il dut fere; et li cevax qui ot senti les esperons l'en porta par mi la presse . . . (10)

Here, just as in the case of Lancelot, surrender to erotic daydream, the retreat into Pleasure and passivity, erases the hero's warrior identity. But just as he is captured, he realises that once dead he will be unable to love his mistress. Killing many of his foes, he captures his father's enemy. But Garin breaks his promise and imprisons his son, who in his underground cell recalls the story of how a sick pilgrim was healed by a glimpse of Nicolete's ankle. The masculine principle embodied in the patrilineal tradition is destructive and repressive; the feminine principle as it appears in Nicolete is therapeutic. But just like metaphor and metonym, the principles of masculinity and femininity have to be in a state of dynamic interdependence if they are to remain themselves. Nicolete takes the initiative and, knotting her sheets together, escapes from her tower-prison. She takes her leave of her lover who displays negative behaviour featuring emotional blackmail, sexual jealousy, threats of suicide and phallocentric self-aggrandise-ment. With the help of the watchman, she escapes, risking the descent into the precipitous moat by symbolically transforming a 'pel aguisié que cil dedens avoient jeté por le castel deffendre' (18) into an alpenstock to help her up the other side. Thus an instrument of war and emblem of patrilineality is transformed by its use into a therapeutic device. Just to take stock for a moment, we should observe that the respective activities of boy and girl have strikingly different values. If we revert for a moment to the idea of writing their behaviour onto the parameters activity/passivity and Pleasure/Reality, we see that Aucassin, whether he is active or passive, remains within the domain of Pleasure, that is, he is dominated by his desire for Nicolete. Nicolete's activity on the other hand is in the Reality/activity quadrant; this is another way of saying that her escape takes her away from her lover and is concerned with self-preservation.[9] In her conversa-tion with the shepherds on the edge of the forest, she leaves a message for Aucassin inviting him to hunt in the forest for a beast (herself) 'qui a tel mecine que Aucassins ert garis de son mehaing'. (20) Just as she healed the pilgrim, so she will heal him. Through the themes of initiative and healing we perceive that a woman, if she is to be fully feminine, must have attributes which are often identified as masculine.

Meanwhile, Aucassin, plunged into a new access of negative passivity on the loss of his mistress, 'dolans et tos soples', is encouraged by a friend to ride out into the forest to seek news of Nicolete. He meets the shepherds and in an encounter of considerable sociological interest learns of the invitation to hunt the magical beast. Here we encounter a topographical transform of the thematic opposition passive/active. The opposition passivity/activity is expressed in terms of a person remaining still while another person moves towards him/her. In leaving her prison to visit Aucassin, Nicolete is defined thematically as active, while her waiting in the forest bower for her lover passes this thematic identity back to Aucassin who has become the hunter at her invitation. The suffering experienced by Aucassin on his journey through the forest is situated by the text in a relationship of equivalence with the suffering of Nicolete scaling the ditch.

Ele segna son cief si se laissa glacier aval le fossé, et quant ele vint u fons, si bel pié et ses beles mains, qui n'avoient mie apris c'on les bleçast, furent quaissies et escorcies et li sans en sali bien en dose lius . . . (17)
. . . les espines . . . desronpent ses dras qu'a painnes peust on nouer desu el plus entier, et que li sans li isci des bras et des costés et des gambes en quarante lius u en trente, qu'aprés le vallet peüst on suir le trace du sanc qui caoit sor l'erbe. (25)

Perhaps this is an index that Aucassin's activity is moving into the activity/ Reality quadrant, since his quest for Nicolete brings him physical pain for the first time.

After hearing of the parallel quest for Roger, the strayed bullock, Aucassin finds his way to the bower, where, in another erotic daydream, which dislocates Desire and Reality, he falls from his horse and dislocates his shoulder. Healed by Nicolete, together they flee the wrath of his father, chivalry and love in ideal balance:

il tint son ceval par le resne et s'amie par le main. (29)

They cross the sea to the kingdom of Torelore where they ask for news of the king and learn that he is lying in childbed while his wife is off at the wars. Aucassin is incredulous and, leaving Nicolete with his horse, goes off with his sword in search of the king, who tells him:

> Je gis d'un fil;
> quant mes mois sera complis
> et je sarai bien garis
> dont irai le messe oir
> si com mes ancestre fist,
> et me grant guerre esbaudir
> encontre mes anemis. . . (30)

Here we encounter, not, *pace* Bloch, an inscrutable nonsense, but the spectre which haunts patrilinearity. Freud, in his essay 'Family Romances', touches upon this when he quotes the old legal tag, 'Pater semper incertus est, mater certissima'.[10] In another of his essays on sexuality 'The Sexual Theories of Children',[11] he refers to the institution of the 'couvade':

. . . one of my female patients happened upon the theory of the 'couvade', which, as is well known, is a general custom of some races and is probably intended to contradict the doubts as to paternity which can never be entirely overcome. A rather eccentric uncle of this patient's stayed at home for days after the birth of his child and received visitors in his dressing-gown, from which she concluded that both parents took part in the birth of their children and had to go to bed.

The king of Torelore is abreacting the repressed anxiety of Garin, Aucassin's father, and his words to Aucassin create a world in which patrilineal structure, purged of its anxieties, imagines a legitimacy founded in the Real rather than in the Symbolic (Lacan's terminology). First, he himself will bear his son, then he will hear mass and go off to war with his enemies, all in accordance with ancestral tradition. Jonathan Culler's thesis in his book *On Deconstruction* is that in patrilineal/patriarchal societies, men compensate for their lack of certainty in respect of biological paternity, and the fears and doubts that arise from this, by emphasising those cultural forms which embody their *symbolic* paternity.[12] The forms that concern us here are war and inheritance, Garin's chief preoccupations being defence of his territory and genealogy. In the battle with the Count of Valens, he says to his son, ' "et saces, si tu le pers, tu es desiretés." ' (8) His son replies that he would rather be with Nicolete, whereupon Garin, like a man whose fear of water causes him to drown, cries: ' "ainçois sosferoie jo que je feusse tous desiretés et que je perdisse quanques g'ai que tu ja l'euses a mollier ni a espouse." ' (8) This can be read as evidence of a neurotic crisis in which the repressed uncertainty of paternity returns in the guise of a willed disruption of genealogy. He would rather see the extinction of his line than countenance a 'mésalliance'. In Torelore, it is the unsureness of biological paternity which is enshrined in the customs of the country. While in Biaucaire both mother and father embodied the Symbolic father,[13] in Torelore the centre of gravity lies in the domain of the feminine. The episode asserts the essential mobility of symbolic sexual identity which we have already observed in the case of the lovers. The king acts out the unconscious fears of patriarchy by taking the female role in childbirth, while his wife leads his army into battle. War, in this playful deconstruction of patriarchal ideology, is not fought with steel but with crab-apples, eggs and curd cheese. The substitution of the sustentive and therapeutic for the destructive stands in a relationship of metaphorical equivalence to Nicolete's transformation of the siege-weapon into an alpenstock and serves as a commentary on the patriarchal institution of chivalry, which, admittedly, takes a back seat in this text. The war between Garin and the Count is unrelentingly brutal. The countryside is ravaged and burned and when Aucassin is captured, the Count looks foward to seeing him hanged. Garin repeatedly promises to burn Nicolete. However, the intertextual clues which mark our story commit it to an implicit dialogue with such texts as *Yvain* and the *Charrette* in which the problem of chivalry plays an important part. Chivalry can be seen as the transformation of war by the principle of therapeutic sustention. The outlawing of missiles (*Perceval*), and the laws of combat, for example, permit armed conflict while reducing mortality. Although for cultural historians ethological criteria may be thought more appropriate as a basis for a rationale of chivalry, here the text proposes the heroine as the narrative focus of the therapeutic theme and it is her narrative double, the queen of Torelore (who also embodies the principle of therapeutic activity), who presides over a resolution of conflict in which there is no killing. The folk-theme of the 'world upside down' here reveals the repressed content of patrilinearity whose structures are transformed by the reversing of sexual polarities and the consequent suffusion of its institutions by the feminine principle. The king *is* the mother of his sons, thus resolving the aporia of legitimacy, and chivalry, that is conflict without mortality, mitigates the patriarchal institution of total war.

Up until this point in the story, the modern reader has been able to maintain his psychologistic frame in reading the characters of the lovers. It is here that the problems begin. Why does the hero in flight from his father suddenly become that father? His response to the mystery of Torelore is to replace it by the very patriarchal institutions whose oppression he had fled. He beats the king and forces him to abolish the 'couvade' and then rides out to slaughter the king's enemies. Patrilineage and total war are re-established. But this is not all. The formerly active and enterprising Nicolete, once she has arrived in Torelore, becomes syntactically as well as diegetically passive. While Aucassin goes off with the king to war, Nicolete

remest es cambres la roine. (31)

The verses in which she pleads to be allowed to remain with her lover highlight her erotic passivity

quant mes dox amis m'acole
et il me sent grasse et mole . . . (31)

Indeed, this sudden reversion to identification with the father is, *pace* Hunt, not a psychologistic but a psychoanalytical event. The son who seemed to have escaped the dominance of the father carries that father within himself. When Aucassin finds himself confronted by a world which challenges the bases of his own psychic economy le Nom/Non du Père is spoken.[14] This is at least one way of semantising the sequence of formal transformations that constitute this aspect of the narrative, i.e. (1) Aucassin active/Nicolete passive (initial attempted wooing of Nicolete) (2) Aucassin passive/Nicolete active (escape and flight from imprisonment) (3) Aucassin active/Nicolete passive (Torelore). The transition from (1) to (2) is psychologistically/metonymically motivated by the commonsense causal relation between circumstances and narrative representations of mental events. The collapse of this motivation in the Torelore episode is signalled by the occurrence of the 'world upside down' motif. This kind of metonymic rupture, which is a defining property of mediaeval and post-modern fiction, has a kind of metanarrative function, in that it collapses the propositionally formulated structure of the narrative into a brief metaphorical instance, a procedure currently known as 'mise en abyme'. An attempted 'repropositionalisation' of the Torelore episode might include something about patrilinearity being defined by the absence of matrilinearity. The text proposes the king and queen of Torelore as role-models for the young pair, models in which the biological and the Symbolic no longer coincide in accordance with the logic of 'either/or'. The king, though in childbed, conserves his allegiance to patrilineal descent, while the queen, who is leading the army to war, nevertheless embodies the sustentive principle in the avoidance of slaughter. The regression of the young pair to their respective patrilineal identities in the face of this parable of conciliation will be slowly undone as each discovers in him/herself the nature of the other.

After three happy years in Torelore, the lovers are kidnapped and separated by pirates — metaphorical agents of the Reality principle. Aucassin returns to take his dead father's place in Biaucaire, and Nicolete, returning to Cartage, discovers that she is the king's daughter. Now we have a fourth instance of the passive/active theme, this time again in its topographical form. Nicolete disguises herself as a male jongleur to set out in search of her lover. Aucassin does not move:

> la se sist sor un perron
> entor lui si franc baron. (36)

In her disguise, Nicolete tells the story of the two lovers and her own history. Aucassin's reply is passionate but passive:

se li dississciés qu'ele venist a mi parler . . . ains l'atenc, ne ja n'arai fenme si li non . . . (38)

Nicolete goes away 'a le maison le viscontesse' her adopted mother, the vicomte being dead, and having re-become herself, sends the vicomtesse to fetch Aucassin, who comes to her, and the next day they are married. This is, everyone agrees, delightful, but does our aesthetic pleasure have a correlate in textual structure? Here, the activity/passivity theme is embodied mainly topographically, Nicolete goes to Aucassin, then he goes to her, then they get married. Now, anthropologically speaking, the instance of the mapping of socio-sexual structure onto topography which is most relevant to this moment in the text is that of marriage-custom. Here the relevant opposition is patrilocal/matrilocal.[15] When eldest son inherits from father, the future wife leaves her home and goes to the house of the bridegroom (the marriage of Conrad and Aliénor in *Guillaume de Dole* is an example of this); when descent is held to be from mother to daughter, the bridegroom goes to the bride's mother's house, where he can replace the dead father (examples of this are plentiful in folktale, the literary domain par excellence of the matrilineal: for example the young hero sets out, kills a dragon to win a princess in marriage and, on the death of her father, becomes king of her country). Seen in this light, Nicolete's quest has a paradoxical double value. As a 'male' in search of a spouse, it is implicitly matrilocally oriented; as a girl going to the home of her husband to be (this is a story about marriage from the start), it is oriented patrilocally. As for Aucassin, his passivity, formerly a negative attribute, has been transformed in this new context into a positive attribute of patrilinearity. This is passivity situated in the 'passivity/Reality' quadrant. Nicolete's quest can thus be seen either as a sort of 'montage' of two logically mutually exclusive social institutions, or as an 'Aufhebung' of contradictory terms, a symbolic marriage of masculine and feminine in their social avatars. Like the king and queen of Torelore, each of the young pair shows an aspect normally associated with the opposite sex, Nicolete takes the active role in courtship and Aucassin is marked by the 'passivity' associated with patrilocal marriage-custom. We have only to remember our own marriage custom to understand how deep this urge for synthesis goes: the wedding happens at the bride's home, under the aegis of mother although the bride is given away by father. Then the pair leave for a short holiday in a place which is ideally the home of neither set of parents, to return, at last, to a new home, often chosen by the husband. The metaphorical interlude of Nicolete's quest is followed by an explication into narrative sequence of the elements of the pair matrilocal/patrilocal. Nicolete returns to the house of her adopted parents of whom the text opts to delete the father,

> car li visquens ses parrins estoit mors. (38)

It is to this house of women that the vicomtesse invites Aucassin to come and the prose of the story concludes with her words, in which the reconciliation of competing modes is consummated in the story's action:

Aucassins, or ne vos dementés plus, *mais venés en aveuques mi* et je vos mosterai la riens el mont que vos amés plus, car c'est Nicolete vo duce amie, *que de longes terres vos est venue querre.* (39)

The subject-matters of the story, parents and children, sexual love, violence, quest and trial, marriage are not only narrative commonplaces but also (and this is why they are narrative commonplaces) the central mysteries of our life, which we feel and experience but do not understand. As Spitzer reminds us, the mediation between feeling and thinking, between affect and concept, is what literary criticism is all about. While the prestige of literary text lies in their power to move us, that is to change significantly the way we feel and think, we all know that any attempt to map poetic structure onto propositional discourse is fore-doomed to failure and this in turn makes us anxiously aware of the inaccessibility of our experience to rational description. This anxiety should not lead us to deny the primal authenticity of our encounter with the text, or to displace its affective charge into activities that enhance our sense of mastery while debilitating us as readers.

Notes

1. R. Howard Bloch, *Etymologies and Genealogies* (University of Chicago, 1983), pp. 178–9.
2. Tony Hunt, 'La parodie médiévale: le cas d'*Aucassin et Nicolette*', *Romania*, 100 (1979), p. 380.
3. Kevin Brownlee. 'Discourse as *Proueces* in *Aucassin*', *Yale French Studies*, 70 (1986), p. 181.
4. Leo Spitzer, 'Le vers 2 d'*Aucassin*', *Modern Philology*, 48 (1950–51), p. 12.
5. Kaspar Rogger, 'Etude descriptive de la chantefable *Aucassin*', *ZRP*, 70 (1954), p. 16.
6. 'Intentional' is used here in its phenomenological meaning to denote that the structure is 'about' something, that its modalities are those of seeking, desiring and perceiving.
7. All references to Mario Roques's *Aucassin et Nicolette* (CFMA, Paris, 1977).
8. See, for example, the entries for 'Principe de Plaisir' and 'Principe de Réalité' in J. Laplanche and J.B. Pontalis, *Vocabulaire de la Psychanalyse* (Presses Universitaires de France, Paris, 1967), pp. 332–9.
9. The idea here is to define the space through which the narrative moves in terms of plus and minus values of two parameters in the following way:

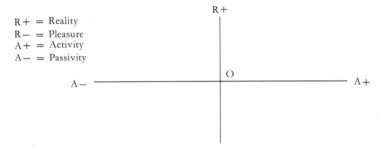

R+ = Reality
R− = Pleasure
A+ = Activity
A− = Passivity

In the upper right-hand quadrant, where both Reality and activity have positive values, we can place Nicolete's escape from prison; in the lower right-hand quadrant, where Reality is negative (i.e. where Pleasure dominates) and activity positive (i.e somebody is doing something) we can, for example, place Aucassin's combat with Bougar de Valence. In the upper left-hand quadrant, where Reality dominates but where someone is doing nothing, we could put Nicolete waiting in the forest for Aucassin, while in the lower left-hand quadrant, where Pleasure and passivity are joined, we could place Nicolete's passive erotic fantasy in Torelore. This is simply a schematic way of representing the interplay between the themes of activity/inactivity and Reality/Pleasure within the text.
10. See Penguin Freud, ed. Angela Richards, Vol. 7 (London, 1977), pp. 217–26.
11. *Ibid.*, pp. 187–204.

12. Jonathan Culler, *On Deconstruction* (London, 1983), pp. 60–1.
13. The 'Symbolic father', as opposed to the biological father, is, in psychoanalysis, that agency which initiates the child into the Symbolic, the world of linguistic exchange, and confers a social identity on him.
14. This is Lacan's pun which refers to the interdiction uttered by the Symbolic father against the pleasure-seeking instinct of the child and especially against the child's yearning for identity with the mother's body.
15. See for example Robin Fox, *Kinship and Marriage* (London, 1970), pp. 84–5.

Villon's Three *Ballades du Temps Jadis* and the Danse Macabre

Kenneth Varty

Ever since I first saw a fifteenth-century wall-painting of the *danse macabre* it seemed obvious to me that Villon's *Ballade en vieil langage françois* drew some of its inspiration from the *danse macabre* tradition, a point made from time to time by some (but surprisingly few) of Villon's editors, translators and commentators. When scholars do point this out, it is usually without any attempt to explain how Villon may have conceived or visualised the dance. For example, Rychner and Henry observe that 'C'est vraiment le *sic transit gloria mundi* illustré par la Danse Macabré, à laquelle Villon revient achevant ainsi le développement commencé au huitain 39.'[1] Even Kada-Benoist (whose study of these three *ballades du temps jadis* is a particularly fine one) says simply: 'la troisième ballade . . . (reprend) ainsi la tradition de la danse macabre'[2] without explaining just what that tradition was likely to have conjured up in Villon's mind. But when scholars do recall it in some detail, it is usually in a way that is at least a little misleading — for example (Rychner and Henry): 'le thème de la Danse Macabré, où l'on voit la Mort saisir et emmener dans sa ronde aussi bien le pape que le laboureur, la reine que la chambrière . . . prend ici sa forme traditionelle. Villon met en mouvement les personnages représentés sur les fresques de la danse des morts [. . .] comme il avait pu les voir au cimetière des Saints Innocents.'[3] This is a little misleading because, in the wall-paintings at the Holy Innocents, there was no queen, nor chambermaid, nor indeed any woman. And it was not *la Mort* which seized those who danced there, but *un mort*, — in all probability a mirror image of each living dancer. In addition, it is probable that Villon *saw* the *danse macabre* more as a *procession* than as a *ronde*.

Eminent scholars have for some time drawn attention to the qualities which unite these three *ballades du temps jadis*, but none has suggested that they are united in part by Villon's particular use of *danse macabre* material.[4] Furthermore, no scholar who has demonstrated the unity of these three *ballades* has explained to my satisfaction why they begin with one which puts the spotlight on women (and lowly-placed women at that) and end with one which, in part, recalls a few features of Old French. In fact, I do not think anybody has asked the question 'why women before men?', and the only explanation I have read for Villon's use of some forms of Old French is that it is meant to be comic, and Villon often uses comedy to release tension after (or while) making a particularly sad or serious point.

First, a few words about my own initial surprise at Villon's treatment of women before men, and in particular at the fact that he begins with the lower end of the social hierarchy. It is, after all, normal in medieval art and literature, reflecting as it does social reality, for men to be presented before women, and upper ranks before lower. Even Villon conforms to this tradition elsewhere in his work, as when he comes to make his bequests, where he starts with his *plus que pere* before he comes to his *povre mere* — and even within this series of *ballades*, in the *ballade en vieil langage françois*, he starts with pope and emperor and ends with *gens privez*. I confess to having had for a long time the feeling that, because Villon treats women in the first of these *ballades* and men in the second, he was leading to a yet higher level in the third, to God. But God is not obviously there. What is obviously there is a glimpse of Society as seen in feudal, hierarchical terms. Was this the climax intended? — women, men, Society?

In an effort to find some answers to these and other questions, I decided to examine the *danse macabre* tradition — texts and pictures — with which Villon might have been familiar, seeking material he might have utilised in one way or another. Now, most of this material has been catalogued, with a different purpose in mind, by Jean Delumeau in his monumental study *Le Péché et la Peur* . . . (1985), and in particular in that part he calls 'Du Mépris du Monde aux Danses macabres' (pp. 44–97).[5] As Delumeau points out, the *danse macabre* is but one form taken by a vast number of texts and visual representations about the vanity of earthly life and values — *contemptus mundi* literature and art. This was often treated in monastic circles well before the flowering of French literature and art in the twelfth and thirteenth centuries, but it flourished especially in the later Middle Ages, probably as a result of the outbreaks of the Black Death which coincided with frequent famines and other disasters associated with the One Hundred Years' War. It went on flourishing not only throughout the fifteenth but also the sixteenth and seventeenth centuries, usually thought of as periods when optimism and pleasure in the joys of this earthly life — no longer regarded as a vale of tears through which Man had to pass — were often celebrated. Under the heading *contemptus mundi* we may group all those sermons and treatises, that vast body of stories and poems, songs and hymns, sculptures and paintings which insist on Man's wretchedness and the vanity of all earthly things, the main point of which was to make men think on things spiritual and seek forgiveness for their sins so that, on the Day of Judgement, they might find favour and be admitted to Paradise. We shall return to this basic aim of *contemptus mundi* thought at the end of this essay.

Important forerunners, then contemporaries of the *danses macabres*, were the processions of the different states and conditions of feudal society which appear in those Latin poems known as *vado mori* poems, the earliest of which are from the thirteenth century, but the majority of which are from the fourteenth and fifteenth centuries. The dramatic cliché 'vado mori' is spoken in turn, with a few lines of verse, by, for example, a king, a soldier, a wise man or a fool.

The earliest (unillustrated) *danse macabre* text proper is, Rosenfeld argues, in Latin, *c*. 1350, from Würzburg.[6] It consists of a series of monologues spoken first by a pope, then an emperor, then a cardinal, and so on as each is made to join in a funereal dance. A mid-fifteenth-century manuscript kept at Heidelberg contains a more elaborate form of this poem which Rosenfeld also attributes to the fourteenth century.[6] This is made up of dialogued quatrains with Death personified addressing representatives of the different social conditions and states (also beginning with a pope and an emperor).

The earliest *danse macabre* text in *French* to come down to us, and one that we can be sure Villon knew well, is the one that was painted on the walls at the church of the Holy Innocents in Paris. This text was in the form of *huitains* and painted alongside (probably immediately beneath) the dancers to which they referred, in the winter of 1424–25. The earliest manuscript version of the Innocents' painted text is dated 1429,[7] but it is a Latin translation of the French mural text, and was translated by Matthieu de Clémages who taught at the Sorbonne and died in 1434.[8] The earliest and perhaps best known *printed* version of the Innocents' mural text is in the book printed by Guyot Marchant in Paris in 1485.[9] He tells us that the text and the woodcut illustrations which accompany it were copied from the walls at the Holy Innocents. A translation was made into Catalan directly from the painted text by Miquel Carbonell in 1497. In the introduction to his translation, Carbonell attributes the French text to the learned doctor and chancellor of Paris called 'Johannes Climachus, sive Climages' — probably a muddled form of the name Matthieu de Clémages, author of the Latin translation of 1429.[10] John Lydgate also translated the Innocents' painted text into English during his stay in Paris between 1426 and 1431.[11] When a *danse macabre* was painted on the cloister walls of St Paul's Cathedral in London soon after 1430, the text accompanying it was Lydgate's translation of the Innocents' *huitains*. Twelve MSS of Lydgate's translation have come down to us.[12] Sixteen French MSS reproducing the Innocents' *huitains*, mostly from the fifteenth century, also survive.[13] Marchant's 1485 printed version of those verses was augmented in a new edition of 1486.[14] This in its turn was taken over by later French printers including Pierre le Rouge and Antoine Vérard. There are in fact 15 different printed editions dating from the period 1486–1500, all reproducing Marchant's 1486 text.[15] Clearly the mural paintings and verses of the church of the Holy Innocents were seminal, being nationally and internationally known in a relatively short time.

It also appears that many other murals took those of the Holy Innocents as their model, and no earlier murals are known. Delumeau maintains that, of the 110

Plate 1. *Detail from Simon Marmion's 1458/9 altarpiece of St Omer.*

Mors oium serno: mors sceptra ligonibus equat: Diffimiles fili cōdicōne trahis
Vado mori: mors certa quidem: nil certius illa. Hora sit incerta: vel mora. vado morir.

Vado mori: quid amem quod finem spondet amarum: Cuius inanis amor non amo. vado mori.

Le mort
Vous qui vivez: certainnement
Quoy quil tarde ainsi dancerco:
Mais quant: dieu le scet seulement
Aduisez comme vous feres.
Dam pape: vous commenceres
Comme le plus digne seigneur:
En ce point honore seres
Aux grans maistre est deu lonneur

Le pape
Hee: fault il que la dance mainne
Le premier: qui suis dieu en terre
Jay eu dignite souuerainne
En leglise comme saint pierre:
Et cóme autre mort me viet querre
Encore point morir ne cuidasse:
Mais la mort atout maine guerre
Peu vault hőneur que si tost passe

Le mort
Et vous le non pareil du monde
Prince et seigneur grāt emperiere
Laisser fault la pomme dor ronde:
Armes: sceptre: timbre: baniere.
Je ne vous lairay pas derriere
Vous ne pouez plus signorir.
Jen maine tout cest ma maniere.
Les filz adam fault tout mourir.

Lempereur
Je ne scay deuant qui iapelle
De la mort: quansi me demainne
Arme me fault de pic. de pelle:
Et dnn linseul ce mest grant paine
Sur tous ay eu grādeur môdaine:
Et morir me fault pour tout gage.
Quest ce de mortel demainne.
Les grans ne lont pas dauantage

a. iii

Plate 2. *The pope and the emperor from Marchant's 1485 edition of the Innocents'* danse macabre.

known visual representations of the dance, all postdate those of the Innocents. The three best known in France after 1425 are at Ker-Maria in Brittany (usually dated *c.* 1460); La Chaise-Dieu at le Puy (*c.* 1470); and La Ferté-Loupière (*c.* 1490). Outside France there were those painted in London (*c.* 1430); others in Basel (*c.* 1440), Lübeck (1463), and in Berlin (1484).

It is abundantly apparent that the *danse macabre* tradition on which Villon drew was, first and foremost, the text and the murals at the Innocents. *But later texts and pictures cannot be set totally aside in case they had an earlier, as yet untraced circulation or reputation.* This cannot be over-emphasised. We know, after all, about some *danse macabre* material that has been lost such as, for example, the dance of death which was performed at the church at Caudebec in 1393,[16] and the dramatised version that was enacted before the Duke of Burgundy in Bruges in 1449.[17] Then there is a tantalising glimpse of a *danse macabre* which, to the best of my knowledge is unknown to both *danse macabre* and Villon scholars alike, and may be dated 1459. This forms part of an altarpiece painting by Simon Marmion. Archives tell us he was commissioned to make and paint an altarpiece in 1458, and that it was in place in 1459 on the high altar of the Abbey of St. Omer.[18] Of this altarpiece (a retable) two wings survive in the Picture Gallery of the Dahlem Museums in West Berlin. Between them they tell ten important episodes in the life of St Bertin, five on each wing. On the right wing, the third episode shows St Bertin with four noblemen kneeling before him as they take their vows as monks of the Benedictine Order. They do this in an unidentified cloister. On the walls of this cloister, in the background, we see a *danse macabre* and, furthermore, the *huitains* which appear beneath each dancer. (Plate 1) (The arcades in Guyot Marchant's woodcuts are perhaps explained by the way one sees two pairs of dancers through the cloister arches. (Plate 2)) Since we know of no cloisters *danse macabre* in France earlier than 1458 we may guess that these details were inspired by the wall-paintings at the Innocents. But pre Villon, there were cloister paintings in London and in Basel; and post Villon, in addition to the murals already mentioned, there were others at Berne and Füssen and elsewhere in Germany, paintings which could reflect a much earlier tradition, and of which we have detailed records.[19] Very late and very remote is an early seventeenth-century Polish *danse macabre* which depicts the dance in a completely unique manner and which I reproduce because of its uniqueness — and because, to the best of my knowledge, it too is unknown to *danse macabre* and Villon scholars alike.[20] (Plate 3) It is unique, I think, in depicting two rings of dancers, one male (on the outside) and one female (on the inside). It is also unique in showing at the corners of the centre arena original sin (Adam and Eve) and its consequence, the price to be paid (Christ on the cross); and the ultimate destination of all sinners, Paradise or Hell. Usually, if these subjects were referred to at all (and they usually were), original sin came at the beginning of any 'processional' representation of the dance, and Christ, the Resurrection, the Day of Judgement, Heaven and Hell were at the end. But this Polish painting is typical in its depiction of the hierarchy (i.e., the highly placed are at the top, the lowlier at the bottom) and in its left-to-right (or clockwise) portrayal of it — but the precise order and representation of social classes and professions differs quite a bit.

Anticipating part of the argument I will be unfolding, I would point out that, in some ways, Villon's *Ballade des Dames du temps jadis* seems to anticipate the women's circle described in anti-clockwise fashion; the *Ballade des Seigneurs* . . . , the men's circle; while his *Ballade en vieil langage françois* corresponds in *some* ways to the corners of the central arena here. But there are lots of important differences.

As I have said, the *danse macabre* tradition on which Villon is most likely to have drawn was first and foremost the one represented on the walls at the Holy Innocents, best preserved in Guyot Marchant's 1485 reproduction of both texts and paintings. Here the *danse macabre* begins at the top of the Church's hierarchy with a pope, then at the top of the state's hierarchy with an emperor. It proceeds downwards through the ranks keeping for quite a while to the alternating pattern Church/State. It continues with cardinal/king, patriarch/constable, archbishop/knight, bishop/squire and abbot/bailiff. The pattern then breaks with the pair astrologer/bourgeois, but is quickly restored with canon/merchant, chartreux/sergeant-at-arms and monk/usurer. It is then broken again with physician/lover and lawyer/minstrel, but finally restored with parish priest/peasant, cordelier/child and, lastly, cleric/hermit — fifteen couples all told, thirty living dancers. Besides noting that the clergy take precedence over the laity, one also notes that nobles come before commoners and that *all* the figures are male. This, I emphasise, is Marchant's supposedly faithful reproduction of the Innocents' *danse macabre* made in 1485.

There were, then, 60 figures in the dance because each of the dancers listed above is led into the dance by a spectral form of himself. It is not Death personified that calls each representative of a social class or condition into the dance, but another beyond-the-grave form of himself. This is often made clear in the paintings or woodcuts and, less frequently, by the text itself. As Chaney writes: 'The original idea was, no doubt, to present a living figure along with another showing what it would look like soon after death. For instance, the Emperor says "Armer me fault de pic, de pelle/Et d'un linseul . . ." and, sure enough, his dead companion does wear a shroud and does carry a pick and shovel. (Plate 2) The basic idea seems to have been to hold up to the living a mirror in which they could see their future state.'[21] As the *premier mort* says in Marchant's text: '. . . regardés nous . . . comme sommes, telx serés vous.'[22] And, as Huizinga puts it, imaginatively: 'The indefatigable dancer is the living man himself in his future shape, a frightful double of his person. "It is yourself" said the horrible vision to each of the spectators . . .'.[23] In some later woodcuts which copy fifteenth-century paintings of *danse macabre* scenes, one sees that the dead form of a dancer is so recently dead that much of the body below the head is still clothed

Plate 3. *Early seventeenth-century Polish* danse macabre, *oil on wood.*

in flesh. For example, the breasts of a queen are still visible in the 1649 woodcut which is supposed to copy the queen as she appeared in the Basel *c.* 1440 mural painting.[24] (Plate 4)

Let us now turn to Villon's *Testament* and the three *ballades du temps jadis.*

It is the third of these *ballades*, the one in 'Old' French, which most obviously reflects something of the Innocents' *danse macabre*. It does so by its all-male cast; putting clergy before laity; pope before — yet alongside — emperor; emperor before king; and nobility before commoners. But it differs in a number of ways, in particular by presenting the whole of the Church's hierarchy in an abbreviated form — from pope to *cilz servans* (i.e. the *convers*, the humblest of the Church's social strata) in the first *huitain*, before presenting the whole of the State's hierarchy, also in abbreviated form (but less abbreviated) — from emperor to *gens privez*, represented by *heraulx*, *trompetes* and *poursuivans* in the rest of the poem. This presentation also differs by concentrating on the upper strata of the two hierarchies — clerical and lay; and by converting all the corpse-like, mirror images into the one powerful poetic image, *autant en emporte ly vens.*

After the *ballade en vieil . . . françois* we are immediately drawn into an abbreviated summing up of the *danse macabre*, in *huitain* 42:

> Puis que papes, roys, filz de roys
> Et conceus en ventres de roynes
> Sont ensevelis mors et frois . . .

after which Villon includes himself as a *povre mercerot de regnes*. Here it is interesting to note that in some mural paintings which post-date those at the Innocents (but not in those at the Innocents), the painter of the murals ended the procession of dancers with a portrait of himself. For example, this was done in the cloisters of the Dominican Abbey in Basel, *c.* 1440; and also in the cloisters of the Dominican Abbey in Berne, *c.* 1515.[25] (Plate 5)

Then, in *huitain* 43, Villon presents us with a *povre viellart*. A poor old man, usually a *laboureur* or a *bawr*, is also commonly depicted towards the end of some *danses macabres*.[26] (Plate 6) Furthermore, the verses show that he is one of the very few who *had* expressed a wish to join the dance. In Marchant's text he begins by saying 'La mort ay souhaité souvent/Mais volentiers je la fuisse . . .'. Villon's *povre viellart* wants death so much that he contemplates suicide — but pulls back (ll. 431–6). In the *Testament* we learn that the *povre viellart* was, when young, famous as a *plaisant raillart*. Whatever a *povre mercerot de regnes* may mean, it clearly indicates a little merchant of some kind — and a merchant takes sixteenth place in the Innocents' *danse macabre*.

Plate 4. *Merian's 1621 copperplate etching copy of the c. 1440 Basel mural of a queen being led into the dance.*

Todt zum Maler:

Hans Hug Klauber laß Malen stohn/
Wir wöllen auch jetztmals darvon:
Dein Kunst/ Müh/ Arbeit hilfft dich nit/
Wann es geht dir wie ander Leut:

121

Hastu schon grewlich g'macht mein Leib/
Wirst auch so g'stalt mit Kind vnd Weib:
Hab GOTT vor Augen allezeit/
Wirff Bensel hin sampt dem Richtscheit.

Plate 5. *Merian's 1621 copperplate etching copy of the c. 1440 Basel mural of the painter of the murals being invited into the dance.*

Le mort

Paſſes cure ſans plus ſongier:
Je ſens quettez abandonne.
Le vifz le mort ſolies mengier:
Mais vous ſeres aux vers dōne.
Vous fuſtez iadis ordonne
Miroer dautruy: et exemplaire.
De vous fais ſeres guerdonne.
A toute painne eſt deu ſalaire.

Le cure

Veille ou non il fault que me rende
Il neſt homme que mort naſſaille.
Plꝰ de mes parroſſiens offrende
Rauray iamais: ne funeraille.
Devant le iuge fault que ie aille.
Rendre compter: las doloreux:
Or ay ie grant peur que neſaille.
Qui dieu quitte bien eſt eureux.

Le mort

Laboreur qui en ſoing et painne
Auez veſcu tout voſtre temps:
Morir fault ceſt choſe certainne
Reculler ny vault: ne contens,
De mort deues eſtre contens:
Car de grant ſouſſy vous deliure,
Approuchiez vous ie vox attens
Folz eſt qui cuide touſiour viure.

Le laboureur

La mort ay ſouhaite ſouuent
Mais volentier ie la fuiſſe:
Jamaſſe mielx fiſt pluye ou vent
Eſtre es vignes ou ie fouiſſe:
Encor plus grant plaiſir y priſſe
Car ie pers de peur tout propos.
Or neſt il qui de ce pas yſſe.
Au monde na point de repos.

Plate 6. *The priest and the peasant from Marchant's 1485 edition of the* danse macabre.

Villon's *povre viellart* seems to have been *quite a wit* (Bonner's translation)[27] in his earlier days. John Fox translates an *amusing jester* and, in his commentary he writes: 'for three stanzas Villon tries to interest himself in this pathetic figure of an old clown . . .'.[28] A wit, a jester, a clown. As I pointed out early in this essay, some *vado mori* poems ended with the fool; and when Marchant came to augment the Innocents text in 1486, he added the *sot* at the very end. The fool also features at or near the end in other pictorial *danses macabres*, for example the one in Basel, *c.* 1440.[29] But what really interests me here is what I believe could be Villon's use of *danse macabre* mirror imagery; for it seems to me that, after drawing himself into this tail-end of the dance as *a poor pedlar of words* (this is John Fox's translation of *povre mercerot de regnes* following the arguments of Rychner and Henry,[30] and is the meaning which makes most sense to me), he follows this, I think, with another picture of himself, a kind of mirror image. He who is a poet, a word-merchant, and was once a wit, a jester, a clown is now a *povre viellart*.

In that part of his study of Villon the man and his milieu, Siciliano writes: 'Ecolier dévoyé, peut-être clerc tombé *in profundum malorum*, il "se délectoit à farcer" . . . Il était dans l'esprit . . . du Sot, on du Galant sans souci.' And he points out that all the references to Villon made in the last half of the fifteenth century and in the first half of the sixteenth century portray him as 'un joyeux vaurien . . . qui jouait des farces . . .'. He also reminds us of a number of lines in his poetry which speak of the wit, the jester and the clown, and suggest links with the *Galants* or the *Enfants sans souci*.[31] This formerly witty, jesting, clowning Villon portrays himself in the *Testament* as prematurely old, very old. He has suddenly entered old age (l. 171); he is a *viel, usé roquart* (734); he has an old man's voice (735); he is *failly, plus noir que meure* (179). He implies that he is dying (728) and that his body (though a poor offering) is ready for the worms (843). Like the *povre viellart* who now has to beg because of straitened circumstances (429–30), Villon too had to wander about penniless (98, 180). Like him, the former fool and funny man who can now say nothing that pleases (438), the poet too displeases by what he says ('Ceste matiere . . . Ennuyeuse est, et deplaisante', ll. 265–8).

It is these and other parallels which make me think that the *povre viellart* who was once a *plaisant raillart* is none other than Villon, a kind of mirror image of the former *gracieux galant, plaisant en faiz et en dis* which he has ironically added to his own *danse macabre*, decrepit old age being seen as a form of death. (One recalls Siciliano's apt comment, 'l'époque qui n'a pitié pour rien [. . .] ne peut concevoir le respect pour l'homme près du tombeau [. . .] vieillir, c'est déjà mourir').[32]

After the *povre viellart* come *ces povres famelettes qui vielles sont* and for whom *la belle heaulmière* speaks. She too provides a mirror image of herself as she once was, beautiful and desirable, contrasting this with her present ugly, disgusting appearance. It is as if a female body just buried has returned to join Villon's *danse macabre* into which she leads her former, youthful self. Particularly telling, it seems to me, is the fact that she is seen naked, like the *momies* of the *danses macabres*. She is *seche, maigre, menue* (491). Her thighs are all skin and bone and mottled like sausages (*mottled sausages* is Bonner's translation).[33] She describes her face as *pally, mort et destain* (515). N.B., *mort*. Indeed, she laments the fact that *Viellesse felonne et fiere* (457) has killed her so soon — *killed* is how I gloss *abatue* in her question to *Viellesse*: 'pourquoi m'as tu si tost abatue?' (458). Especially meaningful, it seems to me, is the line

quelle fus, quelle devenue   (488)

('what I was, what I have become' is John Fox's translation).[34] This is surely an echo of an idea often expressed, and which appears in the introductory lines of the Innocents' text: 'regardés nous: comme sommes, telx serés vous';[35] for the Belle Heaulmière is talking as much to us and to the *pucelettes* (447) and the youthful, pretty *filles de joie* (533–60) as she is to herself. She is holding up a mirror to all young and beautiful women. As she is now, so will they be. The observer of so many representations of decaying corpses read again and again words which in effect said 'what I am, you will be; what you are, I was'.[36] And in Villon's day various versions of the story known as the *Dit des trois morts et des trois vifs* were in wide circulation. At the climax of this story, three well-to-do aristocratic gentlemen unexpectedly come across three decaying corpses in open coffins from which the corpses rise to address their visitors. They reveal themselves as their visitors' future selves. They each tell them 'what you are, we were; what we are, you will be.' This very part of the *Dit des trois morts et des trois vifs* was depicted in stone sculptures and reliefs at the entrance to the Church of the Holy Innocents, and the words spoken by each of the corpses to the three living were carved in verses beneath each of the six figures. This work was executed in 1408 at the command of Jean, Duke of Berry.[37]

As I see it, Villon concludes his *danse macabre* here, with the old prostitute, as good as dead, metaphorically drawing in to the dance a younger, living version of herself. But there were no women, I reiterate, in the Innocents' *danse macabre*, and precious few in any text or series of illustrations before 1461. True, there were four out of 24 dancers in the early *danse macabre* texts in Latin and German which circulated, according to Rosenfeld, in southern Germany from about 1350. There were three out of the 35 depicted in London (*c.* 1430), and as many as eight out of 39 in the Basel murals (*c.* 1440). But even there, there were no prostitutes, no very old women of common stock.[38]

After the composition of the *Testament*, women do not seem to have made their appearance in French *danses macabres* until the murals were painted at la Chaise Dieu (*c.* 1470). Two are brought into it there. In 1486, however, encouraged by the success of his 1485 printing, Marchant published an augmented version of the Innocents' dance, adding ten more male figures to the procession, and creating the first known *danse macabre des femmes*, for which the poet Martial d'Auvergne provided a text. As far as I can make out, six women were included in this first all-ladies dance, but it soon expanded to nine. Here a *vielle demoyselle* makes her appearance, but there is still no prostitute.[38]

Let us return to the three *ballades du temps jadis* and, in particular, to the first two of them. As I see it, Villon's *danse macabre* begins here and, surprisingly really, with women. Even more surprisingly, it begins with women of common stock, with *prostitutes*, just as it will end. Does he, in this way, employ yet another *danse macabre* mirror image? — famous courtesans of ancient times/a famous prostitute of contemporary Paris.

The ascent from the bottom to the top of the social hierarchy in the *ballade des dames du temps jadis* is not, of course, rigorously logical. Flora, Archipiade and Thaïs were thought of as ravishing beauties of common stock; Echo was no less ravishing but had better morals. Heloïs seems to have been very desirable too, and at first far from chaste. She was of moderately good pedigree (being a canon's niece) and became something of a leader (as an abbess). We then climb to royal heights with a queen or two; hover a little, even slip a little if Harembourgis was only a countess. As for *Jehanne, la bonne Lorraine*, here we have a woman of uncertain beauty, not thought of as being sexually desirable, and a mere shepherdess who climbed nevertheless very high to be associated with a king and to lead great captains to great achievements. And she was well on the way to sainthood by the time Villon composed this *ballade*. We then come to the Virgin, of the humblest of origins but whom Villon describes later in the *Testament* as *princesse*, as *Dame du ciel*, *regente* and *emperiere*. With her we undoubtedly reach the top of the ladies' ladder.

The *Ballade des Seigneurs* begins at the top and with the Innocents' number one personality, a pope. There then follows a king, then two dukes. It is as if we have begun to descend through the ranks of royal laity but, relatively late in the first *huitain*, we are jolted back to the king's position (with Charles VII) and then, with the refrain, to the pope's equal, the emperor. The second *huitain* keeps us in the second rank with three kings before returning with the refrain to the first rank, to the emperor. The third *huitain* lets us slip just the once, to a king before returning with the refrain, yet again, to the position of emperor. The *envoi* lets us get quite a bit further down the social hierarchy, down to the fourth rank if we go by the order established at the Innocents, to Claquin, identified as a constable. Only then do we climb back to the emperor via a count and a duke. It is as if the dancers make a number of false starts, returning four times to the emperor's position. At last, however, with the *ballade en vieil françois*, they are ready to do the dance properly, and then they do it at relatively high speed — and yet again in *huitain* 42, slowing down with the entry of Villon himself, going slower still when the *povre viellart* joins in, and coming to a halt with the Belle Heaulmière in her twofold role. Seen like this, the *ballade en vieil françois* seems to play a pivotal role in — as I see it — Villon's *danse macabre*. Pivotal but not climactic as I had felt it might be? Or is there more to it yet? And why in 'old' French? Does an elusive, missing meaning have something to do with the fact that these *danses macabres* were often set between, on the one hand, textual or pictorial accounts of the first mortal sin and, on the other, atonement, resurrection, judgement, heavenly reward or hellish punishment? These dances were, after all, but one of the many kinds of literature and art meant to lead erring or simply unthinking mortals to repentance and salvation. The text of the Innocents *danse macabre* contained the essence of these didactic points, and one of the dead says, near the beginning:

> Entendez tous que vous dis,
> Jeunes et vieux, petis et grans;
> De jour en jour selon les dis
> Des sages vous allez mourans . . .
> Tous les vivans . . .
> De ce monde seront passés
> En enfer ou en paradis . . .[39]

If Villon were making use of *danse macabre* material in the way it was commonly used, somewhere here in the three *ballades* or in the *huitains* which follow there should be something about life beyond the grave. But there is not. It is as if Villon could see nothing beyond death and decomposition — except the reading of his will.

This is perhaps the moment to recall the curious time-sequence of these three *ballades*. As with the climb upwards in the first of them, this is not rigorously logical. In the *ballade des dames* it begins in the distant past and ends, with Joan's death, in 1431. The *ballade des seigneurs* is mostly about men who (where identifiable) died between 1456 and 1461 — the very present as far as Villon was concerned. In the *envoi*, however, there seems to be a wavering and a slipping back into the past, while, in the final repetition of the refrain, we fall back into the distant past. Could it be that Villon brings us to the present, to the brink of the future, only to pull back because he could see no future beyond the grave? This is where I find Kada-Benoist's very fine study especially relevant; for in it she traces the gradual or rapid disintegration of several basic elements which characterise these three poems, including space, time, theme, logic, characters and the poetic *I*. She concludes: '. . . toutes nos recherches jusqu'ici semblent bien appuyer l'hypothèse que le *Testament* est un système rigoureusement construit dans lequel chaque élément de départ se trouve progressivement détruit, désagrégé, pour faire place au néant.'[40] Although I disagree with some of the finer detail in her argument, and am not totally persuaded by the final generalisation, it does seem to me that Villon brings us here to the edge of a precipice down and beyond which there is but nothingness.

The *danse macabre* is recalled again much later in the *Testament*, in *huitains* 160–5. Gabriel Bianciotto read a paper before the French Department in the University of Glasgow in the early 1980s in which he argued that these particular *huitains* strongly suggest that Villon was a non-believer. He pointed out the fierce irony which, in his view, revealed a man who doubted the existence of a God who might preside over a just Day of Judgement. If this is true, we could argue that Villon's *danse macabre* is indeed framed — but distantly, loosely — by thoughts about his sinning and repenting, and by final judgement. (For thoughts about sin and repentance, see especially ll. 105–12). Though I was not convinced by Gabriel Bianciotto's view of *huitains* 160–5, I am struck by the fact that the only powerful resurrection and judgement imagery I have discovered in the *Testament* is about being judged and restored to life on this earth. The first eleven *huitains* tell how Villon was imprisoned by Thibaut d'Aussigny and released, in effect, by King Louis. Lines 82–4 view that period of imprisonment as a kind of death, and release from it as a kind of resurrection:

> Lors que le roy me delivra
> De la dure prison de Mehun
> *Et qui vie me recouvra. . .*

Confirmation that Villon was thinking about resurrection at this point is to be found in the next *huitain*, 13, ll. 99–100, where he writes about the appearance of the resurrected Christ on the way to Emmaus. The story of Diomedes and Alexander which soon follows (*huitains* 17–21) also seems to me to be another image about death and resurrection on this earth. Instead of being put to death by his judge, Diomedes is released to a further period of life in which he makes good, we are told.

The more I weigh up the evidence, the more it seems to me that it was the here and now in which Villon believed. Does he not, as he joins the *danse macabre* of his own creation in the role of a *povre mercerot de regnes*, say that he does not much mind dying an honest death provided he has *fait ses estrenes*? ('had my day' is John Fox's translation).[41] And does not the decrepit old prostitute bringing up the rear of this dance urge the young and active women of the streets 'prenez à destre et à senestre'?

Jean Delumeau writes: '. . . l'attrait du macabre risquait de fourvoyer les hommes du temps [. . .] dans deux directions finalement opposées, l'une et l'autre, au message religieux initial. Le premier de ces chemins sans issue était la complaisance pour les spectacles de souffrance et de mort [. . .] on a abouti à des scènes volontairement malsaines de tortures, d'exécutions et de carnages [. . .] on a glissé à la délectation sadique. Le macabre a fini par être exalté pour lui-même . . .'.[42] Villon clearly did not go down this road. Pity, regret, sadness, compassion characterise all he wrote about death and suffering. Delumeau continues: 'La seconde évasion hors des sentiers indiqués par l'Eglise a consisté dans le retournement du *momento mori* en *momento vivere*: puisque la vie est si brève, hâtons-nous d'en jouir; puisque le corps mort sera si repoussant, dépêchons-nous d'en tirer tout le plaisir possible, tant qu'il est en bonne santé.'[42] As I have already indicated, this is where I think the *danse macabre* led Villon. Did he not say for himself:

> Mourray-je pas? Oy, se Dieu plaist;
> Mais que j'aye fait mes estrennes,
> Honneste mort ne me deplaist . . .

and of *la belle heaulmière* he writes:

> Ceste leçon icy leur baille
> La belle et bonne de jadis . . .
> Prenez à destre et à senestre
> Car (mortes) n'ont ne cours ne estre
> Ne que monnoye qu'on descrie.

There was, however, a time when I thought Villon had a deep trust and faith in God and His love, and that it was the *ballade en vieil françois* which pointed to this. It seemed to me that the ascending line which traced, in the *ballade des dames*, the different kinds of love one might experience was already pointing to this. Villon begins with physical love that could be bought (Flora, Archipiade and Thais); pure love (Echo); passionate sexual love followed by love of God (Heloise); short-lived carnal love ('la royne qui commanda que Buridan/Fust geté en un sac en Saine'); the enduring, faithful loves of Berte, Bietris, Alis and Harembourgis; the love of country, king and God that inspired *Jehanne la bonne Lorraine*; the maternal, divine love of the Virgin. I am not aware that any particular kind of love is celebrated in the *ballade des seigneurs* unless it be the love of power and prowess, war and conquest. But in the *ballade en vieil françois* the refrain (even if it had become something of a proverb in Villon's day) surely recalled that great psalm of David's, the one we number 103, from which the *ballade*'s central image came. At the heart of this psalm David says: 'For (God) knows we are but dust, and that our days are few and brief, like grass, like flowers, blown by the wind and gone forever.' Surrounding this image are some of the most positive thoughts about God and His love — thoughts relevant to the *danse macabre*'s message. 'He forgives all my sins. He heals me. He ransoms me from Hell. He surrounds me with lovingkindness [. . .] My youth is renewed like the eagle's. He gives justice to all who are treated unfairly. He is merciful and tender to those who do not deserve it [. . .] full of kindness and love [. . .] He has not punished us as we deserve for all our sins . . .' We can guess how Villon would have loved to believe this; how, if he did believe it, it was comforting to him and relevant to his *danse macabre*. But before he could believe that 'the lovingkindness of the Lord is from everlasting to everlasting', he had to believe that the Lord was indeed in His heaven.

As Villon's *danse macabre* slows down and finally halts with the *belle heaulmière*'s advice to the *filles de joie*, we realise that Villon (as he portrayed himself in the *Testament*) had no faith in the love of women. If he celebrates the love and beauty of legendary courtesans in the *ballade des dames*, he is bitterly ironic about the favours sold by the women of the Paris he lived in. Pessimism and bitter irony colour his views on women's love. But it seems to me that the most pessimistic note of all is struck in the *ballade en vieil françois* (possibly alongside an optimistic one, if an allusion to Psalm 103 and the everlasting lovingkindness of God was intended; deliberate ambiguity is a common characteristic of Villon's poetry). When Villon recalls (even comically) some of the features of Old French, might he not be holding up yet another *danse macabre* mirror to the living language he uses in his poetry? When one thinks about his legacies, the only ones that have any substance, the only ones he really owned and could give away, are the poems he leaves to a few individuals — one recalls in particular the ballad-prayer he leaves to his mother; and then, when one thinks of it — the whole of his poetry, which he leaves to posterity, to us. Yet, even as he left it to us, it probably occurred to him that the very language in which he was composing would also age and die. May he not have created in the *Ballade en vieil langage françois*, a kind of *momie* which leads Poetry into the *danse macabre*? If so, could a poet be more pessimistic?[43]

Bibliography

On the Danse Macabre
Texts
1. Marchant, Guyot; 1485. *La Danse macabre de 1485, reproduite d'après l'exemplaire unique de la Bibliothèque de Grenoble et publiée sur l'égide de la Soc. des Bibliophiles Dauphinois.* Préface de Pierre Vaillant (Edns. des 4 Seigneurs, Grenoble, 1969).
2. Marchant, Guyot; 1486. *La Danse macabre, reproduction en fac-simile de l'édition de Guyot Marchant, Paris, 1486.* Notice par Pierre Champion (Edns. des 4 Chemins, Paris, 1925).
   Texts, Translations and Studies
3. E.F. Chaney, *La Danse macabrée des charniers des Saints Innocents à Paris* (text and translation of Marchant's 1486 text, with good introduction) (MUP, Manchester, 1945).
4. Gert Kaiser, *Der Tanzende Tod* (Insel Verlag, Frankfurt, 1982) (text and translation into mod. German of (i) Marchant's 1485 text (ii) *Der Doten Dantz mit Figuren*, anon., late 15th century (iii) *Der Baseler Totentanz* as reproduced in book form with woodcuts in 1649 (iv) *Der oberdeutsche vierzeilige Totentanz* as reproduced in the Heidelberger Blockbuch of 1465, and (v) *Der Berner Totentanz des Niklaus Manuel*).
Studies
5. R. Bohm, *Der Füssener Totentanz* (Füssen, 1978).
6. E. Breeda, *Studien zu den lateinischen und deutschsprachigen Totentanztexten des 13. bis 17. Jahrhunderts* (Halle, 1931).
7. J.M. Clark, *The Dance of Death in the Middle Ages and the Renaissance* (Glasgow, 1950).
8. S. Cosacchi, *Makabertanz; Der Totentanz in Kunst, Poesie und Brauchtum des Mittelalters* (Meisenheim am Glan, 1965).
9. J. Delumeau, 'Du Mépris du Monde aux Danses macabres' in *Le Péché et la Peur* (Fayard, Paris, 1983), pp. 44–97.
10. H. Kirchenhoff, *Der Totentanz zu Babenhausen* (A.H. Konrad Verlag, 1984).

11. H. Kirchenhoff, *Der Wondreber Totentanz* (Munich and Zürich, 1976).

12. L.P. Kurtz, *The Dance of Death* (New York, 1934; Slatkine reprints, Geneva, 1975).

13. H. Rosenfeld, *Der Mittelalterliche Totentanz. Entstehung, Entwicklung, Bedeutung*, 3rd edition (Cologne and Graz, 1974).

14. J. Saugnieux, *Les Danses macabres de France et d'Espagne, et leurs prolongements littéraires* (Lyon, 1972).

15. W. Stammler, *Der Totentanz. Enstehung und Deutung*, (Munich, 1948).

16. P. Vigo, *Le Danze macabre in Italia*, 2nd edition (Bergamo, 1901).

17. P. Zinsli, *Der Berner Totentanz des Niklaus Manuel in den Nachbildungen von Albrecht Kauw (1649) herausgegeben und eingeleitet* . . . 2nd edition (Verlag P. Haupt, Berne, 1979).

On the Three Ballades du Temps Jadis and Their Unity

18. F. Desonay, *Villon* (1st edition, Liège, 1933; 2nd edition, Paris, 1947), pp. 170 and ff.

19. J. Fox, *The Poetry of Villon* (Nelson, London, 1962), pp. 148–52.

20. J. Frappier, 'Les trois ballades du temps jadis dans le Testament de Villon', *Bulletin de l'Académie royale de Belgique*, Classe des Lettres, 1971, 316–41.

21. D. Kada-Benoist, 'Le Phénomène de désagrégation dans les trois ballades du temps jadis de Villon', *Le Moyen Age* (Nizet, Paris, 1967), pp. 262–75.

22. P.R. Lonigan, 'Villon's Tryptych, Verses 329–412 of the Testament', *Neuphilologische Mitteilungen* (1969), 611–23.

23. I. Siciliano, *François Villon et les thèmes poétiques du Moyen Age* (Nizet, Paris, 1967), pp. 262–75.

On one or another of the Ballades du Temps Jadis

24. J. Dufournet, 'Une ballade méconnue de Villon: la Ballade des Seigneurs du temps jadis', *Nouvelles Recherches sur Villon* (Champion, Paris, 1980), pp. 29–46.

25. J. Fox, 'A note on Villon's Ballade des Seigneurs du Temps Jadis', *Modern Language Review* (1960), 414–7.

26. D. Kuhn: an analysis of the *Ballade des Dames du Temps jadis* appears in his *La Poétique de François Villon* (Colin, Paris, 1967), pp. 77–97.

27. G. Paris, comments on the *Ballade des Dames du Temps jadis* in his *François Villon* (Hachette, Paris, 1901), pp. 106–8.

28. L. Spitzer, 'Etude ahistorique d'un texte: Ballade des dames du temps jadis' *Modern Language Quarterly* (1940), 7–22.

Some valuable editorial notes on one or other of these three ballades

29. J. Fox, *Villon, Poems* (Grant and Cutler, London, 1984), pp. 47–56.

30. A. Lanly, *François Villon, Œuvres* (Champion, Paris, 1969), Tome I, pp. 83–94.

31. P. Michel, *Villon, Poésies complètes* (Livre de Poche, Paris, 1972), pp. 72–80.

32. J. Rychner et A. Henry, *Le Testament de Villon*, II, *Commentaire* (Geneva, Droz, 1974), pp. 52–62.

Notes

1. Bibl. item 32, p. 59.
2. Bibl. item 21, p. 304.
3. Bibl. item 32, p. 47.
4. Bibl. items 24–8.
5. Bibl. item 9.
6. Bibl. item 13, pp. 60–6 and 89–92.
7. B.N. fonds latin, ms 14904.
8. Bibl. item 9, p. 91.
9. Bibl. items 1, 3 and 4.
10. Bibl. item 9, p. 91.
11. Bibl. item 3, p. 2. Lydgate says, in the third of his prefatory stanzas:

'I toke on me to translaten al
Owte of the frensshe Macabrees daunce.'

12. *Ibid.*, also p. 2: 'The metres or poesie of this daunce were translated out of the Frensshe into English by John Lydgate, the Monk of Bery.'
13. Bibl. item 9, p. 92.
14. Bibl. item 2.
15. Bibl. item 9, p. 92.
16. *L'Art gothique au Moyen Age*, pp. 361–2.
17. Bibl. item 3, p. 3.
18. Greta Ring, *A Century of French Painting, 1400–1500*, pp. 219–20.
19. Bibl. items 4, 5, 10, 11 and 17.
20. M. Rostworowskiego, *Polaków portret własny* (Warsaw, 1983), illustrations 132–5 and the relevant sections of the text.
21. Bibl. item 3, p. 12.
22. *Ibid.*, p. 15.
23. *The Waning of the Middle Ages* (Pelican Books, 1955), p. 147.
24. Bibl. item 4, section (v).
25. Bibl. item 4, pp. 274 and 350.
26. *Ibid.*, p. 98.
27. A. Bonner, *The Complete Works of François Villon* (Bantam Language Library, New York, 1964), p. 45.
28. Bibl. item 29, p. 58.
29. Bibl. item 4, section (iii).
30. Bibl. item 29, p. 57 and item 32, p. 63.
31. Bibl. item 23, pp. 43–5.
32. *Ibid.*, p. 249.
33. See note 27 above, Bonner, p. 49.
34. Bibl. item 29, p. 61.
35. Bibl. item 3, p. 15.
36. One of the earliest examples was on Peter Damian's tomb (died 1032). The Black Prince's tomb in Canterbury Cathedral bears an inscription which says in effect 'I was once what you are, and what I am, you will be.'
37. See E.F. Chaney, *François Villon in his environment* (Blackwell, Oxford, 1946), pp. 135–6.
38. These statistics are culled from Delumeau, Bibl. item 9.
39. Bibl. item 3, p. 16.
40. Bibl. item 21, p. 318.
41. Bibl. item 29, p. 57.
42. Bibl. item 9, p. 128.
43. An article by Jane H.M. Taylor, 'Villon et la Danse Macabré: "défamiliarisation" d'un mythe' (*Pour une mythologie du moyen âge*, edited by Laurence Harf-Lancner and Dominique Boutet (Paris, 1988), pp. 179–96) presents a rather different approach to the problems discussed in the present paper.

Acknowledgements to Illustrations

Plates 2, 4, 5 and 6 are taken, with kind permission, from G. Kaiser, *Der Tanzende Tod* (Frankfurt, 1983). Plates 1 and 3 are taken, with kind permission, from the photographic archives of the University of Glasgow's Department of the History of Art, and ultimately (Plate 1) from the Photographic Department of the Dahlem Museums, West Berlin, with kind permission, and (Plate 3) from M. Rostworowskiego, *Polaków portret własny* (Warsaw, 1983), also with kind permission.

Form and Meaning in Medieval Religious Drama

Graham A. Runnalls

Medieval drama in France takes many forms. When the word 'form' is used in such a sentence, its interpretation is close to that of the word 'genre', and it is with this use of the word 'form' that I shall largely be concerned. To talk about medieval dramatic genres is hardly an original activity. Indeed, a whole book was devoted to the subject recently, and many critics have contributed to the debate provoked by the issue. The notion of genres is a hotly contested one in many areas of literature; it is no less so in the field of medieval drama. Much ink has been used, not to say spilled, in attempts to decide whether a farce is different from a *sottie*, and whether miracle plays are the same as mystery plays, and so on. And although what follows will not simply set out to provide yet one more opinion on the question, but will look at the problem from a fresh angle, no doubt some of my remarks will have a bearing on the unending debate about the problems posed by classifying dramatic texts into genres.

However, I wish to combine my contribution to the question of genres with the other part of the theme of this colloquium, namely 'meaning'. Indeed, if classifying texts into genres has any value or purpose, it is surely related to the understanding and interpretation of these texts; it must help us to appreciate their real meaning. If a text is described, by its author, its editor or by a critic, as a farce, or as a miracle play, or whatever, this definition may set up expectations in the mind of the reader (or spectator). These expectations will clearly influence his approach to the play, and possibly help to determine his interpretation of the play, i.e. the meaning he finds in it, as well as his opinion of its quality. In other words, if one takes the terms 'form' and 'meaning' in the way I have been using them hitherto, one can say that decisions about the form (the genre) of a text are crucial in influencing one's views about its meaning.

In this paper, I intend to talk primarily about French mystery plays. In particular, I hope to be able to show that the normal definition of mystery plays, and the normal attitude adopted towards them by critics, are, perhaps not wrong, but too limited, too narrow; and that this approach to the genre has led to misleading or unfair literary judgements. Many of the received ideas about medieval drama spring, not from the writings of the medieval period, but from works of nineteenth-century scholars like Petit de Julleville, who in turn influenced the major twentieth-century critics such as Gustave Cohen, Emile Roy, Grace Frank and Omer Jodogne. In the same way as critics like these gave credence to apparently authentic technical terms like *mansion* and *lieu*, which are in fact largely a modern invention,[1] so they helped to predetermine our view of the major genres of medieval drama; it is from them that we have inherited our notions of what a typical mystery play should be like.

What I wish to do is to bypass these modern, widely-accepted opinions, and to go back to the late medieval period itself, in order to try to find out what dramatists and other writers in the fifteenth and sixteenth centuries thought mystery plays should be like. This is not an easy thing to do. It is very rare to come across medieval definitions of mystery plays. However, there are several sources of evidence that one can use to get some idea of contemporary attitudes to this question. First of all, of course, there are the plays themselves, and the titles they were given. If a medieval dramatist wrote a play that he or his scribe called a *mystère*, it would be a very bold twentieth-century critic who would say that the text in question was not a true mystery play. In fact, this kind of blunt dismissal is rare; what one does find more frequently, however, is a modern critic saying that such and such a text is a bad mystery play, or an untypical example of the genre. This latter kind of observation is more subjective and less easy to contradict, but it does nevertheless hinge on the critic's conception of the genre itself. It is therefore important, as a starting point, to examine medieval classifications of plays, via the labels and titles given by dramatists to their plays.

A second source of information about medieval attitudes is provided by the various contemporary descriptions, edicts, decrees, statutes, and the like relating to medieval dramatic texts; though not numerous, these reveal general notions about the ways in which plays were perceived to be grouped.

The third and last type of document I shall refer to is the only attempt that I know of to describe the way in which a mystery play should be written. This comes from one of the *Arts de Seconde Rhétorique*, and casts some surprising, though :incomplete light on the subject.

Having analysed these sources, I shall then compare and contrast what information they give with the views and judgements of some of the nineteenth- and twentieth-century critics I have already mentioned. Finally, I will look briefly at one or two plays, to see how they stand up to description and evaluation in the light of the various opinions discussed.

Before turning to medieval information, however, let us consider modern definitions of the mystery play. One of the most recent is that given by Alan Knight in his book *Aspects of Genre in Late Medieval French Drama*.[2] He divides medieval drama into two main types, historical and fictional. 'Basically the historical genres [to which Knight attaches the mystery play] commemorate a sacred past by reaffirming for the community whatever is "digne de mémoire", while the fictional genres [i.e. farces, *sotties*, moralities] teach lessons in human ethics by presenting examples of conduct both good and bad.' This careful and sensible definition avoids several of the terms used by earlier critics to define mystery plays; but, unfortunately — from the stand-point that interests me — Knight devotes most of his book to discussing the fictional genres. Grace Frank and Gustave Cohen, in their surveys of medieval French drama,[3] either implicitly or explicitly — and usually explicitly — divide the texts they discuss into two sorts, religious and comic. Cohen's book, for example, is physically split into two parts: *le théâtre religieux* and *le théâtre comique*; mystery plays are dealt with under the religious theatre. Grace Frank arranges her book in a large number of chapters; the first 19 deal with various types of religious play; only in chapter 20 does she start to discuss comic drama. Mystery plays are examined in chapters 13 to 19. Both Frank and Cohen, as well as most other critics, accept this major dichotomy between religious and comic drama.

It is obvious, however, that *religious* and *comic* are not antonyms. The opposite of religious is profane or secular; the opposite of comic is serious. But generations of critics never seem to have been unduly troubled by this anomaly. Similarly, Cohen and Frank were not noticeably embarrassed by the fact that several plays they had to discuss were both comic and religious, for example the *Jeu de S. Nicolas*; and they either ignored, or passed very briefly over, plays, like the *Destruction de Troye*, which were neither religious nor comic. As far as Frank and Cohen were concerned, mystery plays were religious but not comic. Now, of course, for many — for most — plays, this definition works perfectly well. But the important point in all this is that those plays which appeared in some ways to be mystery plays, but which did not fit with this definition, were either held to be aberrant or inferior or else were not discussed at all. It is in this way that faulty definitions of genres can give rise to misleading interpretations or evaluations of plays, or even to their neglect.

Let us now turn to medieval information which sheds light on how mystery plays were viewed by medieval writers, and first of all, to the titles given to plays by the dramatists and scribes themselves. According to my calculations,[4] there are 76 surviving manuscripts or early printed books from the fourteenth to the mid-sixteenth centuries containing 'mystery plays' whose title page has survived. Since title-pages are almost invariably the first folios of a manuscript, many others have been damaged or lost; but, as I say, I calculate that about 76 have survived. Here, I must add that I am talking only about plays that critics have considered to be religious and not comic, i.e. so-called mystery plays. Several conclusions can be drawn from an analysis of these titles. First, one notes that no manuscript dating from before the fifteenth century has the title *mystère*; one can infer therefore that the *mystère* is a type of play written and performed in the fifteenth and early sixteenth centuries only. Secondly, and more importantly, one is struck by the fact that these 76 texts offer as many as 26 different types of title. Thirteen of the titles include no reference to any type of play, to what I will henceforth call a 'genre-word'; these simply have the name of the subject-matter of the play, for example *Le Jour du Jugement, L'Incarnation et Nativité, La Nativité*; this group includes virtually all the Passion Plays, for example *La Passion Nostre Seigneur Jhesu Crist*. Only nine plays, out of the 76, are described simply as *mystères*, for example *Le Mystère du Roy Advenir, Le Mystère des Trois Doms, Le Mystère de S. Quentin*. Seven plays have the name of the subject-matter, without 'genre-word', but followed by *par personnages*, for example *Passion par personnages, Vengeance par personnages, Sacrifice d'Abraham par personnages*. There are nine texts where the word *mystère* is used in conjunction with *par personnages*, for example *Le Mystère des Actes des Apostres [. . .] tout ordonné par personnages, Le Mystère de Job par personnages, Le Mystère de S. Christofle par personnages*. Seven plays are entitled *Vie [. . .] par personnages*: for example *Vie de S. Louis par personnages, Vie de Marie Magdaleine par personnages*. The many remaining titles are extremely varied, often combining two 'genre-words', to which *par personnages* may or may not be added, for example *Mystère et Histoire [. . .] par personnages, Miracle, Livre et Mystère, Vie et Miracle, Vie et Martyre par personnages*.

Several conclusions emerge from these confusing data. First, there was no single 'genre-word' used for these plays in the Middle Ages. At least ten different labels could be used, including *mystère, miracle, vie, histoire, jeu, moralité, livre, passion, martyre, representacion*. Second, that on many occasions, a scribe used more than one of these words to describe a single play. Third, although *mystère* is the most frequent 'genre-word', with 31 occurrences, the item which appears most often in these titles, on 37 occasions, is the expression *par personnages*. This is really the crucial phrase which distinguishes dramatic from non-dramatic literature. In fact, only *jeu* and *moralité* never occur in conjunction with *par personnages*; their dramatic status is unquestioned. But all the other 'genre-words' can be used in Middle French to describe things other than plays, although, to be fair, this is less often the case with *mystère*.

So this brief analysis of the contemporary titles of plays has shown that many of the texts now called mystery plays were *not* so called by their authors; that *mystère* was simply the most frequent among ten different labels likely to be attached to such a play by its author; and that *par personnages* was very often attached to the name of the subject-matter, to form the title of a play.

Further light is cast on the medieval use of the word *mystère* in two contrasting official documents, one dating from the beginning of the flowering of the genre, the other marking its decline. One of the first occurrences of the word *mystère* is found in the letters patent of 1402 in which Charles VI authorised the Confrérie de la Passion to perform plays in public: 'pour le fait d'aucuns misterres, tant de saincts que de sainctes, et mesmement du misterre de la Passion, qu'ilz dernierement ont commencié . . .' This example suggests clearly that mystery plays could be about saints' lives or the Passion, but it is not obvious whether they could only have that kind of subject-matter. In 1548, however, the Parlement de Paris issued an edict which many critics have interpreted as signalling the end of mystery plays in France (though this is not in fact correct). The edict 'deffend de jouer le mystere de la Passion nostre sauveur, ne autres mysteres sacrez'. There is a definite implication here that there were *mysteres* that were not *sacrez*, and that these were not forbidden. This interpretation corresponds with the facts; the Confrérie de la Passion continued performing plays, but they were no longer the sort that had infuriated the Paris Parlement, i.e. the *Actes des Apostres* and the *Mistere du Viel Testament*, which they had organised with great popular success in 1541 and 1542.

The third source of information about what mystery plays consisted of, in medieval eyes, is found in the only one of those numerous texts called the *Arts de Seconde Rhétorique* to deal with drama. Most of these texts, dating from the late fifteenth and sixteenth centuries, dealt mainly with problems of versification and rhyme. One, however, the *Instructif de la Seconde Rhétorique*,[5] devotes several pages to the following subject: 'comme l'on doit composer moralitez, farces, misteres . . .'; this is the subject of its tenth and final chapter. The *Instructif*, dated by its editors about 1472, is written, unusually, in verse, and devotes 14 eight-line stanzas to the composition of mystery plays, or, as the Latin sub-title reads: *pro misteriis compilandis cronicis et hystoriis*. This becomes, in the versified French text:

> Pour faire croniques notables
> Ou hystoires ou beaulx misteres . . .

These words, both in the Latin and in the French, confirm the evidence provided by the titles of plays discussed earlier: *mystères* is just one title among many, *hystoire* and *cronique* being considered as synonyms, provided that the context is, as it is here, drama — *par personnages*.

The rules provided by the *Instructif* cover content, sources, scope, style, language and versification. I will discuss briefly each of these types of rule and relate them, where relevant, to known plays.

The first stanza contains a kind of definition of the genre, though rather a vague one; in order to write one of these plays, the author says:

> L'on doit par ornees manieres
> traicter une grant chose . . .

In other words, a mystery play must deal with a major, not a trivial, subject, one of considerable significance or scope; moreover, its treatment must be complex, ornate. The only other detail provided by way of definition relates to the play's sources; the play must be based on:

> vrayes translations entieres.

Mystery plays, therefore, are not original fictional creations; they must be based on known facts handed down by trustworthy sources.

There is no difficulty in showing that all surviving mystery plays correspond to this admittedly vague definition. Even the shortest ones deal with a major subject: a Biblical episode, a saint's life, an important event from ancient or recent history. And all have sources that critics usually have no difficulty in tracing, whether the Bible, Latin or French miracles of the Virgin or saints' lives, or Roman, Greek or French history.

The author of the *Instructif* then devotes three stanzas to the question of the number of characters in the play; these, he says, must be worked out in advance. In particular, it is essential that characters of important social standing should appear accompanied by the appropriate number of attendants, servants, soldiers and so on. This recommendation is certainly followed in virtually all mystery plays, for example Jesus with all twelve disciples, Lucifer with a team of devils, Caiaphas with a dozen Jews, Pilate with several Roman soldiers, saints with numerous disciples. Indeed, it was by giving speaking roles to these secondary characters who, in the earlier plays, were mere walk-on parts, that the later mystery plays grew to be so long.

Versification is the next topic discussed. The main point which the author of the *Instructif* makes here is that, at certain emotional high-points in the plays, i.e., to use his own words, when the action contains 'regretz et plainctes, ou louenges', the dramatist must use complex verse forms like the *lai* or the *virelai*. Moreover, he must give them in their complete form, with the right number of stanzas and refrains. Again, anyone who has read any of the later fifteenth- and sixteenth-century mystery plays will know how complex their versification regularly is. Many of the technical skills of the *grands rhétoriqueurs* found their way into mystery plays; indeed, many of the authors of mystery plays were famous *grands rhétoriqueurs*.

The last major section of this part of the *Instructif*, the final eight stanzas, concerns the use of language. The author writes:

> L'on doit donner langaige
> a chascun selon la personne;
> se c'est de clergie personnaige,
> parler de clergé on luy donne.

This rule about the use of a linguistic register appropriate to the character is then extended from the clergy to the nobility, to bourgeois and merchants, to the fiery young and to the worthy old, to labourers, masons, carpenters and smiths, to sailors, to soldiers, to servants.

It seems, at first glance, somewhat surprising that over half of the *Instructif*'s section on mystery plays should be devoted to this question of appropriate linguistic register. But, again, the texts of the mystery plays themselves show clearly that all authors attempted to do what is recommended here. Jehan Michel's fishermen disciples have lengthy conversations using lots of technical sailing and fishing terms.[6] Eustache Mercadé's inn-keeper boasts of the twenty different types of wine he sells (including an English wine).[7] And there is no lack of examples of learned clerics using learned language: in Gréban's *Passion*, the discussion between the young Jesus and the Doctors in the temple lasts for over a thousand lines.

However, this last recommendation is more than just a linguistic or stylistic one: it also implies a type of content that we might now prefer to call local colour. Moreover, it urges mystery play writers to incorporate into their plays characters from all levels of society, including the lowest, and realistic scenes where the audience can witness the everyday existence of these ordinary people.

It emerges from this close analysis of the *Instructif* that its author saw mystery plays as follows. They are plays which dramatise a subject of great importance and which are based on authentic written sources. Their treatment is on a large scale, both in terms of the complexity of the versification and of the number of characters. These characters reflect a wide range of social classes and the scenes in which they appear show the audience a portrayal of real life.

It goes without saying that this description clearly distinguishes mystery plays from moralities, *sotties* and farces. It is also undoubtedly the case that all these features are found in the plays we now call mystery plays.

But there are problems and surprises in the *Instructif*'s description, especially as far as its omissions are concerned. The most striking of these is the total absence of any reference to religion. Nowhere does the author of the *Instructif* call mystery plays religious plays. He does, in effect, call them historical plays, in that they must be based on recorded sources, and not on the dramatist's imagination. In this, the *Instructif* is clearly right.

The other omission relates to comic and vulgar material; the author of the *Instructif* does not mention it explicitly. One could say, however, that its presence is implicit in his recommendation that lower-class characters should use appropriate language. It is undoubtedly the case that many, but not all, mystery plays contain scenes of crude brutality and vulgar humour, often mixed together. In this respect, as elsewhere, the author of the *Instructif* reveals himself to be something of an idealist, or even a purist. This aspect of his character also comes out in his description of the farce. He is all in favour of farces being based on what he calls a 'joyeuse matiere'; but he warns strongly against all forms of bad language, 'ort langaige'. Not many farces appear to heed his warning!

In conclusion, I would say that the author of the *Instructif* provides an accurate but somewhat purist view of the mystery play. At least, that is what emerges from a comparison between what he recommends and the texts that have survived.

If we now return to the approach towards mystery plays adopted by nineteenth- and twentieth-century critics, we can see that they too, at times, can be accused of being purist. For they insist on the religious nature of mystery plays (not mentioned in the *Instructif*) and seem to use this fact as one of the criteria invoked in evaluating mystery plays.

If one examines the writings of scholars like Grace Frank, Gustave Cohen, Omer Jodogne or Emile Roy, one can see that they all tend to agree about which are the best mystery plays to have survived; there is a generally accepted hierarchy of quality. At the top of the tree come the Passions of Gréban and Michel; towards the bottom come plays like the *Passion de Semur* and some of the plays in the composite text now called the *Mistere du Viel Testament*.

However, a problem does arise in connection with nineteenth- and twentieth-century evaluations of mystery plays: this is that very few plays are actually analysed and assessed in depth. One might expect this in general surveys of medieval French literature as a whole; but even in manuals of medieval French drama, only a few are looked at in detail — and usually the same ones. Of course, part of the reason for this is the length of the texts, and the limited number of modern editions. Even in such invaluable works as Petit de Julleville's two-volume study of the *mystères*, which lists and describes all the mystery plays known to have survived when he wrote in 1880, what one gets is only the externals of the texts: date, length, number of characters, details of performances and sets, résumés of the plot. Petit de Julleville, like many others, refrains from anything but the most general, and subjective, critical assessments. Moreover, these critics often repeat each other, both in the texts they choose to describe more closely and in the opinions they express. For example, a play described by Petit de Julleville in 1880 as showing 'une prolixité et une crudité de détails' is characterised by Grace Frank in 1958 as 'crude and prolix'. Coincidence alone can hardly explain such uniform evaluation. The plays that receive the most thorough attention in the manuals are the twelfth- and thirteenth-century plays, the four-teenth-century *Miracles de Nostre Dame par personnages*, and just a handful of the long mystery plays, especially the three big fifteenth-century Passion Plays of Mercadé, Gréban and Michel, and a few saints' plays.

I have no wish to disagree with the favourable opinions that all critics have expressed about Gréban's and Michel's Passion Plays. What I am more concerned about is those plays that these critics consider to be bad, for it is from these judgments that one can deduce what they think a mystery play should and should not be.

One very revealing article in this respect is Omer Jodogne's essay on what he calls 'La Tonalité des mystères français'.[8] He discusses a number of religious plays — the usual ones — praising some and attacking others, and concludes by saying: 'Dans l'ensemble, la gravité et le lyrisme des mystères s'accommodent très humainement de ces scènes brèves où l'on concède un brin de poésie profane et quelque comique familier', but he rejects any broader comedy or any crudity or violence. For him, and for most other critics, the criteria defining the tone of a

good mystery play are 'gravité et lyrisme'. These the three main Passion Plays
have in large measure.

But, in discussing the *Passion de Semur*, Jodogne observes that in this play, as
distinct from the others, 'il y a du comique acceptable — et du comique burlesque,
sans parler de la grossièreté dont il faut souligner l'excès — grossièretés qu'on a
jetées à pleines brassées dans ce drame religieux'. Jodogne finds the presence of
these elements 'avilissante'.

What one can see in Jodogne's aesthetic of the French mystery play is nothing
less than a continuation of the traditions of the French Classical theatre of the
seventeenth century — no mixing of comedy and tragedy, the superiority of
tragedy, no juxtaposition of the grotesque and the sublime, preference given to
purity and uniformity of tone, to '*bienséance*'. But this approach, whether con-
scious or unconscious, is manifestly anachronistic; not surprisingly, many
mystery plays do not live up to the demands and expectations of such critics; they
are thus dismissed as bad plays, or else not discussed at all. What is needed is an
attitude to mystery plays which eschews anachronistic aesthetic demands, and
which takes the plays as they are, evaluating them on their own terms and bearing
in mind contemporary notions of the theatre. In other words, we need a different,
or at least a broader, conception of the genre of the mystery play.

The final part of this paper will consist of a discussion of a little known mystery
play, which the few critics who have mentioned it have dismissed as worthless,
and which certainly does not match up to the conception of the genre as revealed
in Jodogne's article discussed above. I would nevertheless argue that it is a good
mystery play.

The play in question is *Judith et Holofernès* (henceforth referred to as *Judith*); it
is one of the plays that make up the compilation known as the *Mistere du Viel
Testament*. No manuscripts of any of this 60,000-line work survive, but it was
printed in Paris in 1500 and several further editions were published towards the
middle of the sixteenth century. It is not a single unified work, but a sort of
anthology of plays written, no doubt, towards the end of the fifteenth century.
The complete collection was performed in Paris in 1500 and again in 1542. The
Judith play was also performed, separately, at le Puy in 1585; it is just under 2,500
lines along and probably took about three hours to perform.[9]

The main outline of the play follows the Apocryphal book of *Judith*, and relates
how the faith of one woman succeeds in overcoming overwhelming military
force. Holofernes, leading the Assyrian armies of the self-declared God
Nabugodonosor, threatens to destroy any Jewish cities that refuse to acknowl-
edge the divinity of Nabugodonosor. His armies completely destroy one city and
frighten another into capitulation. The priests who rule Béthulie, where Judith,
an attractive widow, lives, also contemplate surrender, until she furiously berates
them for their cowardice and says that she alone will save them. She dresses in
her finest and most alluring robes and visits Holofernes' camp. He is immediately

attracted to her, and Judith pretends not to be hostile to his barely concealed desires. After a feast, during which Holofernes gets progressively drunk and aroused, he retires to his tent with Judith, thus provoking his fellow officers and his personal man-servant to make numerous sarcastic barbed comments. As soon as he is lying in bed, undressed, relaxed and waiting for what the medieval French farce authors euphemistically call 'cela', Judith grabs his sword, cuts off his head, puts it in a bag, and leaves the Assyrian camp using the safe-conduct Holofernes had already given her. The death of Holofernes gives heart to the Bethulians and demoralises the Assyrians who flee.

The main theme of the play is obviously the triumph of the true faith over the infidel (although in an Old Testament play, the true faith is the Jewish faith), and demonstrates how prayer and a firm belief in God can give strength to the apparently weak. But there are other, equally important sub-themes running through the play. For example, in spite of the several scenes of battle, the author's intention is to criticise war and war-makers. The Assyrian officers are presented as boasting and egotistical warriors, who are more concerned with getting one over on their fellow-officers than with any religious issues; they view war merely as a way of getting booty and plunder. A late fifteenth-century audience would no doubt sympathise with such criticism; significantly, the pagan armies are often referred to as 'compagnies'. Yet, paradoxically, a little sympathy — only a little, though — is shown for the wretched foot-soldiers who do the officers' dirty work and suffer the consequences of wounds and death.

Thus far, the play sounds serious, but there are major comic dimensions to the text. The overweening pride of Nabugodonosor, which sets the action in motion, is cleverly reflected not only in the pompous words of his opening speech, but also in its exaggeratedly complex versification; he uses complicated verse and rhyme schemes, including internal rhyme, *rimes enchaînées* and *rimes annexées*. The full battery of the *grands rhétoriqueurs* is brought into play, but for comic effect. Different metrical forms are used to highlight Judith's prayers and her vitupera-tion against the weak Jewish priests. Comedy is also evident in passages where Holofernes tries to court Judith. He attempts to use gallant, courtly language to disguise his frankly sexual urges, and Judith defends herself by using similar ambiguous courtly phrases; the whole scene is a parody of courtly banter. Holofernes' man-servant is a eunuch, and his series of amusing, sarcastic and lascivious asides, as he sees his master appearing to win the affection of Judith, extend over much of the latter part of the play and deliberately puncture the potential high drama of the scene.

The few modern critics who claim to have studied this play have nothing good to say about it. Petit de Julleville says: 'On y observe une prolixité et une crudité de détails qui montrent jusqu'à quel point, dès le XVe siècle, le mystère était atteint du défaut par où il devait périr. A tout moment, le poète semble se parodier lui-même. A aucune oeuvre mieux qu'à *Judith* ne convient la réputation de trivialité grivoise attribuée à tort à tous les mystères.[10] This is an extremely revealing judgement, which demonstrates perfectly what I have called the purist and anachronistic view of mystery plays. Grace Frank, as I mentioned above, repeats Petit de Julleville's words: 'The *Judith* play, despite the potentialities of the story, is crude and prolix'.[11] Even the editors of the text, Rothschild and Picot, can only find the versification worthy of favourable comment.[12]

I think that these critics are wrong. Even objectively, there is no way that a 2,500-line play containing virtually all the action of the *Book of Judith* can be called prolix, certainly not when compared with the Gréban and Michel Passion Plays, each of which contains about 30,000 lines. But the main reason why these critics are wrong, I would contend, is that they are basing their opinions on a false view of the mystery play. As we have already seen, they want 'gravité' and 'lyrisme'; they don't want humour, violence, satire or sex.

Yet if we compare the *Judith* play with the definition provided by the author of the *Instructif*, we will find that it corresponds very well. It is obviously based on a subject of great importance, which is treated in a complex and at times ornate manner. It is based on authentic sources; one cannot get more authentic, in this context, than the dramatisation of a book of the Bible. The play includes a wide range of characters, with those of the highest social rank accompanied by the appropriate number of *figurants* — priests, soldiers, servants, etc. Each type of character speaks of subjects, and in a fashion, typical of his background. For example, the priests pray eloquently, Nabugodonosor speechifies pompously, Judith adapts her language to suit the role she is playing, sometimes praying fervently, sometimes hurling insults at the Jewish priests, sometimes bandying courtly clichés with Holofernes. The officers of the army, for their part, use large numbers of technical terms; at one point, the four of them mention, between them, 52 different items relating to armour and weapons. The miserable foot-soldiers curse, swear and insult each other. In sum, the play shows a whole world of people and an equally wide range of linguistic registers. The author of the *Instructif* would have no reason to condemn this play.

Moreover, its success can be attested by more objective criteria, namely by its survival itself, its three recorded performances over 100 years from the end of the fifteenth century to the end of the sixteenth, and by the fact that it was printed and published in several editions in the course of the sixteenth century.

I would conclude that *Judith et Holofernès* is a good example of a typical late medieval mystery play; contemporary evidence also suggests that this is the case. So what *is* a typical late mystery play? What kind of definition corresponds to the texts known to the late Middle Ages as *mystères*?. It has to be a much wider definition than that used by the ciritics I have mentioned above. Putting aside questions of staging techniques and versification, and just dealing with subject-matter and tone, I would say that mystery plays were dramatisations of a slice of life from the past, of events recorded by the collective memory of the people (not just the intellectuals), and which, in the opinion of the dramatist, were of significance for himself and his public. There were no limitations as regards tone or style. Mystery plays could thus be serious or comic, though they were often both. They could be grave and lyrical; but they could also be violent and crude. The authors certainly had no preconceived notions about uniformity of tone, and were happy to mix the tragic and the comic; any suggestion to the contrary is anachronistic. Within the mystery play form, one can observe numerous variants. Gréban's *Passion* is serious, sensitive, thoughtful, with some light and pleasant touches. The *Passion de Semur*[13] is full of contrasts, heavy and allegorical at times, at other times, vulgar and crude. The *Passion d'Arras* is learned, earnest and rather tiresome. The *Mystère du Roy Advenir* is in many respects more like a dramatised romance. *Judith et Holofernès* resembles a melodrama, with strong comic undertones. All of these texts, whether they are pedestrian or works of genius, are perfectly acceptable mystery plays. Critics who try to reject or dismiss some of these are failing to appreciate their instrinsic qualities and are guilty of adopting an excessively narrow view of the genre.

And now, a post-script. As I was re-reading this paper, it suddenly crossed my mind that the person in whose honour these essays are published has written one of the best concise surveys of medieval French literature. I thought I had better check up to see what John Fox has to say about mystery plays, in case any of my strictures against modern critics hit the wrong target.

I was relieved — but not surprised — to discover that I had no need to worry. In rounding off his section on Passion Plays, John Fox concludes: 'In the end, they impress by the industry they display, not by any genius'.[14] I would agree, on the whole, with this assessment of the French Passion Plays. However, John goes on to say, with the modesty which we know is characteristic of him, 'But this, of course, is no more than the literary judgement of a twentieth-century manual. For thousands of spectators these plays may well have constituted a unique and intensely moving occasion.' I think he is right.

Notes

1. G.A. Runnalls, '*Mansion* and *lieu*: two technical terms in medieval French staging?', *French Studies*, 25 (1981), 385–93.
2. Alan Knight, *Aspects of Genre in Medieval French Drama* (Manchester University Press, Manchester, 1983).
3. Grace Frank, *The Medieval French Drama* (Oxford, 1958); Gustave Cohen, *Le Théâtre en France au Moyen Age* (Paris, 1948).
4. G.A. Runnalls, 'When is a *mystère* not a *mystère*? Titles and genres in Medieval French religious drama', *Tréteaux*, 2 (1980), 23–8.
5. *L'Instructif de la Seconde Rethorique* [*sic*], Preface of the *Jardin de Plaisance et Fleur de Rethorique*; published by Antoine Vérard in 1501; ed. E. Droz and A. Piaget, 2 vols (Paris, 1910 and 1924).
6. Jehan Michel, *Mystère de la Passion*, ed. Omer Jodogne (Gembloux, 1959), ll. 3924–89.
7. Eustache Mercadé, *La Passion d'Arras*, ed. J. Richard (Arras, 1893), ll. 23164–202.

8. Omer Jodogne, 'La Tonalité des Mystères', *Studi in onore di Italo Siciliano, Bibliotheca dell' Archivum Romanicum, First Series*, 86, Part I (1966), 581–92.
9. *Judith et Holofernès* in *Le Mistere du Viel Testament*, ed. Baron J. Rothschild (and Emile Picot), SATF (Paris, 1878–91), vol. 5, ll. 41856–44325.
10. L. Petit de Julleville, *Les Mystères* (Paris, 1880), vol. 2, p. 374.
11. Grace Frank, *op. cit.*, p. 195.
12. *op. cit.*, vol. 5, pp. cxi–cxviii.
13. *La Passion de Semur*, ed. L. Muir, (University of Leeds, 1981); G.A. Runnalls, 'The Evolution of a Passion Play: the *Passion de Semur*', *Le Moyen Français*, 19 (1988), 163–202.
14. John H. Fox, *A Literary History of France: The Middle Ages* (London, 1974), p. 254.

Aspects of Form and Meaning in the Biblical Drama

Lynette Muir

Mais ses oevres en ce beau lieu,
Se paix nous volez ministrer, ·
Par personnaiges demonstrer
Vorrons, en la forme tres belle
Que LE JEU DE DIEU on appelle . . .
Si en verrez le ostention
Afin que ediffication
Fache au poeuple en clere advertence.   (Mons, p. 457)[1]

The *Jeu de Dieu*: the play of God. The phrase from the Mons Prologue reminds us that the medieval approach to the biblical drama is different from that of any other generation, for the medieval attitude to the Bible is different. The Bible is the Word of God but the Word, the Logos, *is* God, the Second Person of the Trinity. So the Bible is the Incarnation of God and the plays are the Incarnation of the Bible, the Word of God.

From the earliest tropes onwards, the biblical drama focussed on the Risen Christ. As the plays developed and performance became widespread and elaborate, the focus was enlarged, but not altered — a move from close-up to wide-angle lens. The Old Testament motivated, prefigured or prophesied the New; the life of Christ — ministry, miracles and martyrdom — provided the pattern for the Acts of the Apostles and the Lives of Saints; Christ's own warnings foretold Doomsday. Christocentricity was the staple of the medieval drama — *Passions, Osterspiele, Autos*, Miracle, Mystery or Cycle play — as it was the staple of the great web of exegesis, apocrypha, sermons and meditations from which the plays were cut out to create a unique cosmic theatre, with a subtle, complex form and a multiplicity of meanings.

Moreover, the authors of the plays took over not merely an exegetical approach to the Incarnation but also a liturgical one. Day by day, week by week, the clergy read and the laity heard the biblical stories, in fixed patterns following the cycle of the Christian Year from Advent to Pentecost and the anonymous, green, feast-flowered Season that followed it.

109

Just as typological associations dictated much of the iconographical form in the visual arts, so in drama the selection and arrangement of material from both Old and New Testaments is dictated by these liturgical patterns which give the Passion plays their characteristic and distinctive form.

The present paper seeks to examine a few examples of the ways in which the medieval playwright and producer interpreted, theatrically, their narrative sources by conflation or amplification of characters and episodes and the use of costume and decor; and particularly how liturgical form and sacramental meaning were used to give an additional dimension to the already elaborately exegetical narrative. I shall begin with a few examples from the first, great biblical play in the French language: the Anglo-Norman *Adam*.

Signs and Sermons in the Anglo-Norman *Adam*

An important clue to our understanding of this text is provided by the (usually mistranslated) title, *Ordo representacionis Ade*. It is not a *Ludus* or *Jeu* and certainly not a *Mystère*. If we compare *Adam* with other twelfth century dramatic *Ordines* such as the *Ordo Prophetarum* or *Ordo de Ysaac et Rebecca et filiis eorum recitandus*, we observe a special stress in the Latin didascalia on the ceremonial and ritual of the performance — location, properties and costumes are all mentioned. In contrast the (equally twelfth-century) *Ludus Danielis* limits its directions to movement on an unspecified area and gives no mention of clothing.[2]

The strong liturgical links of the *Adam* are apparent if we realise that Latin lections, responsories and prophecies make up about a third of the total text; the early *Sponsus* play, in contrast, has about one-third French to two-thirds Latin. The costumes prescribed are also, in some cases, liturgical — Salvator, at the beginning, is wearing a dalmatic. (Iconographically, the Salvator was distinguished as young and beardless and almost certainly here appears rather than God the Father because of the Deuteronomic prohibition against the representation of God which kept the Father out of art till the very end of the twelfth century.) The dalmatic is a liturgical vestment most commonly worn by the deacon, so the question arises — why is Christ not shown here as a priest? Various possibilities may be canvassed: the deacon was especially ordained to read the gospels and preach and the Salvator at the beginning of the play is preaching to Adam and Eve on the subject of marriage: 'Tel soit la lei de mariage' (24). Alternatively, the Salvator is the Logos, the Word, so appropriately dressed like one reading the Word of God. Other reasons could be adduced and there is no way of knowing which, if any, is correct, but it seems certain that there *was* a reason, for later in the play the Figura appears, wearing a stole and evidently acting as a priest, for the scene of the Expulsion of penitents from the church which took place on Ash Wednesday.[3]

The term Figura seems almost certainly to derive from its use in the Epistle to the Hebrews to designate the Son as the figure of the Father: 'figura substantiae eius'. (I, 3) A similar usage occurs in the introductory speech of the *Ste Geneviève Passion*: 'En une digne sepulture;/La fut de Dieu mis la figure' (119–20). This insistence on the creative role of the Son helps to emphasise his redemptive role also — Adam knows that none can help him, 'For le filz qui istra de Marie' (720) and Figura himself knows that there is none to rescue Adam, 'Se moi nen prenge pité de vus' (884).

Sign-language, verbal or visual, is basic to medieval drama and derives of course from the Bible itself. The author of St John's Gospel was perhaps the first writer to use explicit semiotics and it is interesting to notice that the changing of water into wine at the marriage in Cana, which in the Greek and Latin biblical texts is described as a *semios* or *signum* by which Christ manifested his glory (as in the Epiphany, which explains the presence of the Cana story in the lectionary for the second Sunday after Epiphany), becomes in the plays just another miracle: 'Et apres commence le miracle comme il mua l'eau eu vin . . .' (Michel 4989). The use of 'miracle' in this context in the Authorised Version of the English Bible suggests that this was common practice in vernacular texts of the end of the Middle Ages.

Whenever a non-historical or non-traditional element appears in a play it is probably a sign of some kind. For example: Adam and Eve are shown clothed, not naked. Although real nudity was not possible on the stage (especially with Eve being played by a man) the *choice* of covering is surely significant. In this instance it seems likely that the red and white clothes they wear represent their state of glorious innocence. Adam wears a *tunica rubea*. Is this the ordinary tunic of a peasant, or is it rather the tunicle of a sub-deacon, a long garment almost identical with a dalmatic and surely more appropriate in conjunction with Eve's white silk headdress? There are several possible reasons for the choice of colours, and it is worth noting that the same contrast of red and white is used for Cain and Abel.[4]

A different kind of semiotics is provided by the stage direction for the Devil to come and sow thistles in the patch of earth Adam and Eve have been cultivating. In this juxtaposition of two different biblical ideas, the parable from Matthew (III, 24) emphasises the symbolic meaning of the episode as well as the literal consequence of the Fall. 'In the sweat of thy face shalt thou eat bread (Genesis III, 19); a complex web of fruit/bread/eucharist imagery constantly recurs in the three sections of this highly sophisticated and subtle play.[5]

Simultaneous and Synchronic Staging in the Fifteenth-Century Plays

If we turn now to the fifteenth-century plays we find a similar approach to the biblical material, though the inclusion of Latin texts is almost entirely limited to the many sermons and does not form part of the dialogue as in some German plays. The *Eger Fronleichnamspiel*, for example, has many parallels with the *Adam* play, including the use of the name Salvator for the Creator and the alternating of the spoken vernacular text with sung Latin responsories.[6]

While preserving liturgical chants and musical references, the narrative line in the French plays usually follows the biblical chronology which, for the New Testament, involves, of course, conflating the different Gospel narratives. Although the narrative passion poems of the later Middle Ages (which provided the source for many of the dramatic versions) had no problems with this harmonising, the strongly liturgical approach of the dramatists could cause difficulties as in, for example, the sequence of the Christmas narrative. Matthew's Gospel tells of the coming of the Wise Men, followed by the Flight into Egypt and the Slaughter of the Innocents; Luke tells of the Shepherds, then the Circumcision followed by the Presentation in the Temple and the Purification. Logically, the last-named must precede the Flight into Egypt, but liturgically the Flight is part of the Epiphany story read on 6 January, while the Presentation in the Temple does not take place until Candlemas, 2 February, 40 days after the birth.

The English plays, which were mostly tied to a sequential form of staging, were reluctant to separate the Herod material between two guilds so tended to keep it together.[7] This, however, meant the Purification taking place after the Flight into Egypt. The simultaneous staging of the French plays removed the problem, for they could retain the liturgical and logical order and simply find an excuse to delay Herod's ordering of the Massacre of the Innocents until after the Purification. In Semur, where the author also interlaces the sequence of scenes in Rome between Octavian and the Sybil, Herod wonders why the Magi have been so long coming back and a pilgrim to Jerusalem who has conveniently found his way to Herod's court says cheerfully, 'les troys roys sont ja en leur regne;/Alé sont par autre païs' (3296–7). Herod rages. A more original and dramatically skilful handling of the situation is to be found in the Arras play. Herod remarks that, since the Magi have not come back, that is a sure sign they were wrong after all and do not want to admit it. He is only disillusioned when one of his followers who has been present at the scene in the temple tells him how Simeon took the child in his arms 'qui maintenant a maintenu/qu'il est d'Israel Dieu et roy'. Galopin adds fuel to the fire by adding 'Et me doubte que les Juys/En temps advenir ne lui donnent/Vostre regne et ne le couronnent' (4567–8; 4583–5).[8]

The flexibility of the synchronic staging method allows great variety in the organisation of material in the French plays and it is interesting to observe the changes made between an 'original' play, such as Greban's *Passion*, and the versions of it actually staged at Mons or at Valenciennes. Greban himself used the Arras play and was in turn used by Jean Michel for his text of 1486. Subsequently, both Greban and Michel were mined by the compiler of the Mons text: Cohen's superb edition of this shows how the sources were selected, rearranged and conflated, with lines from the two authors being juxtaposed sometimes in the same speech. Moreover, the Mons redactor adds new scenes and characters, especially in the Old Testament episodes. The Flood sequence, for example, owes nothing to any earlier version but reappears fifty years later in the Valenciennes 20 play of 1549.[9] Other changes in the Old Testament section are the introduction of a series of prologues between the scenes (unfortunately we have only the first and last lines of many of them) and a character, *Humain Lignage*, who is involved in the action and also acts as a kind of 'chorus to this history'. A similar handling of given material is observable in the Troyes play (another Greban variant) which also introduces a recurrent character but in this case it is a humorous one — the Sot — who makes comments on the action and often uses contemporary satirical allusions. Such a role, be it *fou*, *vilain* or *rusticus*, though rare in passion plays, occurs in no fewer than eight of the surviving saints' plays, not to mention the character of the ubiquitous and iniquitous Daru, the executioner, in the *Actes des Apôtres* who turns up, boasting of his skill, all over the world whenever an apostle is to be martyred. This kind of 'running gag' technique is also used in the *Passion de Semur*: Noah's bad son, Chaim, is cast out by his father and turns into the Rusticus in which guise, later assisted by a wife, a son and a daughter, he takes an irreverent role in the subsequent play, regardless of the time element, quarrelling with his wife at the Nativity; trying to buy a *Poire d'angoisse* from one of the Sellers in the Temple; and struggling to prevent the apostles from taking the donkey for the Entry into Jerusalem. This cavalier attitude to temporal reality is typical of the plays in which time is never historical. But then the Bible itself is no mere history book. The Gospels are Good News rather than *Vitae Christi*. Rooted in historical time and space (*sub Pontio Pilato*) they may be; biographies they are not.

A different kind of linking of the separate parts of the story is by the doubling of characters or by giving known names to biblically anonymous functionaries: Greban and Michel, for example, introduce Annas and Caiphas into the Nativity sequence as two of the interpreters called in by Herod to advise the Kings on the place of Christ's birth. Semur goes even further, for the underlying structure of this play is the evolution of the Old Law into the New and an important secondary character is the Jew, Damp Godibert, part comic and part serious. He is summoned from the Temple by Herod to speak to the Kings, helps Simeon at the Purification and, thirty years later, still in the Temple in Jerusalem, is involved with the plots of Annas and Caiphas and has the unique role of preparing their Passover meal for them — no other text I know of reminds us that *all* the Jews in Jerusalem were celebrating the Passover that Thursday evening. Godibert also appears occasionally during the Ministry: for example, when Christ talks of the destruction of the Temple, Godibert knows he is referring to his own Body: 'Quant ceste chose adviendra/Nostre loy mout peu se tendra./C'est son corpz, cy com je l'expose;/Plux desclarer ne vous en ose,/Car la chose est pesant et dure' (5718–22). An expositor but part of the action, a Jewish exponent of the disintegrating Jewish law, a member of a comic group representing the Synagogue: in Damp Godibert we have a truly original and dramatically effective character.

Biblical Narrative and Contemporary Reality

All these characters, biblical or dramatic, are made more immediately accessible to the audience by the stress on their humanity: eating and drinking have a considerable place in the plays. The meal as a set-piece is, of course, common in the Gospels, culminating in the Last Supper (see below p. 120), but in the plays the food is introduced, quite literally and specifically, into many other episodes. In Semur, the shepherds have a meal before setting off for Bethlehem and discuss the excellence of the food. (1st Shep.) 'Comme ce lait est espes,/On le tailleroit au coutel.' (2nd Shep.) 'Je n'an mangay oncques de tel;/C'est pour ce qu'il est de brebis.' (Hersent) 'Il n'est pas ainsin que tu dix,/Mes il ya a eufz a foisom,/C'est ce quil fait la liaisom/Et quil l'a ainsin fait espes.' (Semur 2663–70). Hersent is one of the shepherdesses who is left to guard the sheep while the men are away. This is a common feature of the plays — sheep cannot just be abandoned! In Arras the three Kings are given wine and spices by Herod: 'Cy font collation, puis dit Herode.' (3657) Sometimes the meals are related to a biblical datum as when the kings go to the inn from the stable — they are going to have a dream, ergo they must go to bed. In Arras, they have taken the precaution of bespeaking their accommodation beforehand: 'Gauwain, alez nous retenir/Ung hostel pour nous hebergier' (3743–3) and apparently also had dinner at the Inn (there was room for *them*, but then they were Kings) for Gauvain subsequently settles the bill: 'Mon hoste, entendez a moy, ça,/Combien d'argent volez avoir/Pour tout?' (4119–21). It costs them two besants altogether. In Troyes, the scene is given additional realism by naming the inn at which they stay: 'adoncques les dicts trois Roix arriveront au logis du Signe en Bethleen' (I, 6540). Evidently an inn sign was used on the relevant mansion. The Swan was a well-known inn in Troyes. On another occasion the Sot refers to the Auberge de la Licorne (I, 5720), which was near the play-site. In Greban (and Troyes) the time necessary for the Kings to go to sleep is covered by a meal for the servants, and from the Mons accounts we learn they ate 'une piece de mouton' costing four sous (p. 566). All the stage meals for Mons are listed in the accounts and for Herod's feast, when Salome (or, as she is called in Mons, Florence) dances for the head of John the Baptist, the food provided is strictly fish — it is Friday (p. 569). This stress on the observance of the rules of the Church even by actors on the stage becomes even more interesting on the occasion of the Last Supper when the accounts provide for both a real lamb — 'pour ung agneau rosti . . . pour Dieu faire sa Pasque' (16 sous) and also another lamb 'de paste couvert de poisson rosti, mengie [. . .] ou lieu de l'autre ci dessus ad cause du samedi' (3 sous) (p. 571). Since it is not credible that they would have only realised the necessity of not eating meat that day at the last minute (Saturday was a regular fast day), the existence of the two lambs must be for dramatic realism. One to be a *real* paschal lamb, the other so that they can *really* eat it.

Another very common way of staging biblically-derived material is the 'shopping' scene. The prototype is the purchase of the spices by the three Maries found in many liturgical *Visitatio* plays; a similar scene occurs in the *Sponsus* play, where the foolish Virgins rush off to buy oil for their lamps — in vain: 'Dolentas, chaitivas, trop i avem dormit!' (p. 184). The scene of the Maries and the Merchant is unknown in English vernacular drama but common on the continent; in one of the first French dramatic *Passions*, the early fourteenth-century Palatinus, the *Espicier* describes how he has travelled from Salerno and through Auvergne where he has found herbs etc. (1864–8). Mary Magdalen then arrives 'de loing' (1911), and asks for 'un chier oignement precieuz' (1920) and he offers her three boxes full, for which she has to pay thirty pounds (1927). In Arras, they only have to pay 20 besants (compared to 100 besants in Greban, 28296) to have their own three boxes filled with ointment 'cler net et luisant' (21460); earlier in this play, Mary Magdalen purchased an alabaster box of ointment 'fin, net et luisans' for 30 besants (10091). Other examples include Joseph of Arimathea buying the shroud, (Ste Geneviève, Michel and Greban); Nicodemus purchasing the spices with which to anoint the body (Greban); and a very unusual scene from the Arras play in which, during the Last Supper, Christ tells the disciples that he that has no sword: 'let him sell his coat and buy a sword' (Luke XXII, 36). Immediately, the action cuts from the Upper Room to a 'fourbisseur' who describes all the weapons and armour he has for sale (11213–28). Enter Peter and James the Less who bargain for two swords. They are charged eight sous and Peter leaves his cloak in pledge for the money. They return to the Supper and explain 'Lord, behold here are two swords' (Luke XXII, 38). This scene can surely only be justified as a dramatisation of the exchange between Christ and the Apostles, and to explain where Peter acquired the sword with which he is about to cut off Malchus's ear. The change of register, from the solemnity of the Last Supper to the humour of the boasting 'fourbisseur' and back again, is typical of the abrupt variations we have already seen in this play in, for example, the scene between the innkeeper and the messenger of the three Kings (see above p. 114).

Occasionally, the authors draw their liturgical parallels with an equally heavy hand, as in a sequence from the Auvergne *Passion*. Christ meets the disciples of John the Baptist and goes with them into the Temple in Nazareth to say 'nostre office' (710). Inside a 'prestre' orders his fellow to bring the 'livres pour chanter' and then, says the stage direction, 'cantent sicut in secunda dominica' (715). Since Jesus then reads some sentences from Isaiah, including the passage about the blind seeing and the dead being raised (XLII, 7), it evidently means the Second Sunday in Advent when Isaiah is read and the Gospel at Mass describes Christ sending a message to the disciples of John the Baptist to tell John what they have seen: 'the blind see [. . .] the dead rise again' (Matthew XI, 5).

Visual Symbolism: Costumes and Decor

There are a variety of other techniques used by the dramatists to express their
narrative sources·in a theatrical form — the development of biographical details
for characters like Mary Magdalen and Judas in Michel's *Passion* is a notable
example[10] — but the verbal element in the plays is also complemented by the
visual, and the form of the decor and costumes (as has already been noticed in the
Adam play) may have a meaning that is more than simple representation.

The civic plays, for which the most staging information is available, were put
on by the municipality, but actors normally provided their own costumes, so few
references to them occur in the accounts. A few clues do subsist, however, such
as the letter written by Jean Bouchet of Poitiers to the council of Issoudun who
had asked him to direct their passion play. He declines but gives them some
advice, including 'Et qu n'usez tant d'habitz empruntez/(Fussent-ils d'or) qu'ilz
ne soient adjustez/Commodement aux gens selon leurs roolles./Il n'est pas beau
que les docteurs d'escolles,/Pharisiens, et les gens de conseil/Ayent vestement a
Pilate pareil,/Ne a Herod . . .'.[11] If in the light of this comment we look back to
Michel's own directions and also to those in the Mons text, we understand
Michel's reason for specifying certain costumes, most importantly for the
apostles. When first called, they are to be in their 'habits mechaniques' (4265);
Peter, Philip, James and John are fishermen, Bartholomew 'en habit de prince'
(4181) and Thomas is a carpenter — though he is to leave his tools behind when
he follows Christ (4217).

John the Evangelist appears in a white robe as the bridegroom at the marriage
in Cana[12] and James the Less should be 'vestu et habillé pres ou environ comme
Nostre Seigneur' (4406). Traditionally, as the brother of the Lord (here interpreted as cousin which puts him on the same footing as the Zebedees), James was
sufficiently like Jesus for Judas to have to identify Christ to the soldiers at the
arrest by the kiss: 'Ici doit saint Jacques Minor sievyr Jhesus et est a noter que
c'est celui qui lui ressembloit et pour ce doit-il estre habilliét assez pres ainsi que
Jhesus et tousjours en cest estat poursuyr, tant qu'il ara son habit d'apostle'
(Mons, p. 161).[13] The apostles' mantles were apparently *vermeil* at Mons (cf.
p. 292), which would be appropriate when we remember that the liturgical colour
for feasts of apostles is red.

What none of these references tells us, however, is what Christ himself wore,
though it is clear from the above remarks that he is not distinguished from the
rest of the company by any noticeable mark such as that prescribed (at Lucerne)
even for the new-born Christ, who is to be played by a six-month-old child in a
tiny halo with three golden lilies. A similar (but larger) halo is worn by the adult
Christ.[14] Haloes for the apostles are mentioned in York, and a gilded face for the
twelve-year-old Christ in the Temple is prescribed in the Chester plays.[15] In the
latter, the Virgin Mary also appears crowned in the Purification play. In France,
the only time Christ has a gilded face and hands is for the Transfiguration (Mons,

p. 177), and there is no other evidence for such a distinction even in the representation of God the Father. The most likely reason for these differences of approach and form is the very different style of the staging. In England, the audience are very near the actors who may indeed be mingling with the crowd around the pageant. Some kind of distinction then becomes useful especially if (as in iconography) the haloes bear the apostle's name and he also carries his symbol. These would help to identify the individual speaker (there are ten different Peters in the York cycle) and to distance him from the crowd sufficiently to retain the characterisation. The French crimson mantle seems to have more the significance of a priestly vestment, symbolising the new role of the former fishermen (see above p. 116). Whether formal, symbolic or realistic, the costumes in medieval plays are always contemporary and not historical: even God himself, in Heaven, has some resemblance to the pope, appearing often in a cope and a Phrygian cap with tiara. A rare and interesting aural portrayal of God is in the Michel/Mons Baptism and Transfiguration when the Father speaks from Paradise: 'la loquence de Dieu le Pere se peut prononcer entendiblement et bien a traict en troys voyx: c'est asçavoir ung hault desus, une haulte contre et une basse contre bien accordees et en cest armonie se peut dire toute la clause qui s'ensuyt' (Michel 2123). This is clearly meant to represent the Trinity.

A consequence of this counterpoint between stylisation and contemporary reality is the creation of a special dramatic time scale in which the unities of time and space are expanded to eternity and infinity; audience and characters meet at one moment in time: the liturgical present, where the historical event is represented and commemorated; the play is not a recreation of yesterday but a celebration of today.

Angels, Devils and Man's Condition

This Eternal Now, the invasion of Time by Eternity which is the underlying concept of the Incarnation, is kept before the eyes of the audience by the physical presence of Heaven and Hell in the big French plays — a possibility not available to those using small stages or pageants. On stage right, always present visually and often audibly, is a location of beauty and harmony, lights, music, curtains and flowers — the presence of God. Opposite, gaping jaws and evil faces, thunder machines, cannon, quarrelling and smoke remind us of the power of evil. The eternal tug-of-war, eternally portrayed.

These opposing forces may also be represented in actual conflict on the Terran battlefield. Devils tempt Judas to betray Christ or to commit suicide (Greban 17415; 21745); Pilate's wife's dream is devil-inspired as is the tale told by the guards at the tomb (Greban 23372; 31811); the orgy of Humain Lignage before the Flood is organised jointly by the devils and the deadly sins (Mons, pp. 19–22). On the side of the angels, we see (in addition to the prescribed appearances at the

Annunciation or Temptation) angels sent to comfort the Virgin Mary (Troyes II, 6861); Gabriel assisting Christ to disrobe at the Baptism (a well-known motif also in iconography); the Father sending angels to escort Christ on the way to Calvary and even — rather untheologically — to comfort him as he hangs on the cross (Michel 27044–6).

When Adam and Eve or the Foolish Virgins are taken off to Hell by devils, or when angels escort John the Baptist to Limbo, this is not just a stage convenience (though getting bodies off the stage did present problems before the introduction of the proscenium curtain), but a reminder of the medieval belief that every dead soul was escorted by angel or devil, up or down, at death. In Arras, St Michael and Satan quarrel over the soul of the Good Thief and the former wins, leaving Satan to make do with the soul of the Bad Thief; in Greban, Satan gazes in bewilderment at the dead Christ on the cross and wonders where this soul has gone: 'Mais que son ame soit devenue/Je n'en scay rien, n'en quel party' (25867–8). A particularly effective piece of stage business in Michel is the seizing of the soul of Judas: devils stand round the hanging corpse clamouring, but no soul appears because it normally comes out of the mouth (with the breath) and this black soul cannot pass the lips that have kissed Christ. Then the devils rip open the body which has a bag of pig entrails hanging under its robe and seize the soul. Normally the soul was represented by a doll, but in this play the soul speaks as it is dragged off, so the scene must have been played over a trapdoor through which it could emerge (Michel 23987). A similar device is used for scenes of the exorcism of devils which then appear through the trap with a bang, and rush off to hell in a trail of smoke (Mons, pp. 184–5).

This is one of a number of indications of how devils were portrayed on the stage, the most important being the Provençal director's text which describes in detail the construction of a fire-breathing devil's mask.[16] Angels on the other hand are never described in the later plays and it seems likely they were similar to those depicted in iconography. However, the angel who comforts Christ during the Agony in the Garden is not represented in the French plays as carrying a cup, though this is common in iconography,[17] but the angels who minister to Christ at the end of the Temptation may have appeared in a liturgical or ritual form. In Michel, for example, they are instructed by God to take food to Christ: 'Icy descendent les anges de Paradis et aportent une couppe couverte et du pain couvert d'une fine serviette a Jhesus' (3102). The implication here is eucharistic, but in the Harvard Baptism (the first day of the Auvergne Passion) the form is liturgical: it is God who gives the angels the bread to take to Christ and the stage direction states 'tradit panem angellis' a clear reference to Psalm 77 'Et panem caeli dedit eis,/Panem angelorum manducavit homo' (vv. 24–5), still used as a liturgical chant (but perhaps better known nowadays in César Franck's setting of the *Panis angelicus*). Harvard further emphasises this parellel by the angels' description of Christ as the 'Pein vivant'. Moreover, instead of taking the bread directly to the fasting Christ they stop off at the house of the Virgin Mary (in answer to her prayer) and take to him also the supper she has prepared. The two foods, heavenly and earthly, are received with equal joy by him who is both Man and God (Harvard, pp. 124–32).

Angels and devils are not only biblical, symbolic and liturgical (not to mention iconographic); they may also be used dogmatically as in a scene from the Valenciennes 25 play of 1547. Joachim and Anna (future parents of the Virgin Mary), are unhappy because they are childless. An angel announces to each in turn the birth of a child. They meet at the Golden Gate and kiss — a scene often depicted in iconography. They then return home and retire to a curtained bed on the stage, which is immediately surrounded by angels to keep off the devils who seek to arouse Joseph's concupiscence (through which Original Sin would be transmitted to the child.) The dogma of the Immaculate Conception of Mary was not to be promulgated for another three centuries, but it is clearly the meaning of this particular scene.

Staging the Sacraments: How and Why?

A final aspect of form and meaning to be considered is the representation in the plays of the sacraments of the Church. Marriage is indirectly influential in the *Adam* play, which opens with Figura's marrying Adam and Eve: Adam is warned to rule his wife by reason and to show her 'grant amor/grant conservage' (To love and to cherish), while Eve must serve and love her husband and above all be obedient to him (To love, honour and obey), for 'ço est dreiz de mariage' (*Adam* 38). Penance is portrayed in Michel's play: the penitent Mary Magdalen, moved by 'remors de conscience' (12082), makes a confession of her sins in full sacramental form, dividing her actions under the headings of the different parts of each of the Seven Sins, just as the manuals recommend (12082–12253). This also echoes the biblical reference to the seven devils which Christ cast out of Mary Magdalen (Luke viii, 2). The forms of Baptism and Confirmation do not noticeably affect the staging of the Baptism of Christ or the Coming of the Holy Spirit at Pentecost, and Supreme Unction and Ordination are rarely mentioned outside the saints' plays (but see Last Supper plays, below p. 120), though the sacrament of the Mass is recalled in many of the scenes of the Last Supper.

From *Adam* onwards, dramatists used the theme of fruit or bread of life as a leitmotif running through their imagery. In Semur, particularly, this fruit-of-life is explicitly linked to the eucharist. When Charité and Esperance plead with God to release Man from the prison into which he has fallen through his own deeds, God at first hesitates because 'combien que puisse tout despecier et tout faire/Cy ne puis ge pas de moy mesme deffaire/Je, quil suis verite, mentir je ne pouroie,/ce j'estoie menteur, Dieu pas je ne seroie' (1758–61). Having expounded his difficulty in reconciling justice with mercy,[18] God then finds the solution: 'Un paradix terrestre de novel reffairé,/C'est le corps de la vierge ouquel je descendray;/En ce bel paradix je veul estre planté/Et pourter feulle et fruit quant g'y seray enté./A ceulx qui me croiront le fruit abandonnerey,/Et vie pardurable avec moy leur donray' (1786–91). The idea of the two fruits, the old and the new, is found in a number of non-dramatic texts (notably versions of the Holy Rood legends), but the closest to the Semur version is that used by Guillaume de Deguilleville in his *Pèlerinage de l'Ame,* where St Peter offers communion to Adam and Eve from a table set beneath the Tree of Life: 'faire je vous vieng essaier/D'un mes et d'un nouvel menger/Afin que aprés vous jugiés/Quel fruit, le nouvel ou le viés/Vaut mieux et est plus vaillable' (10597–10601).[19]

The next stage, in the plays, is to link the fruit of the tree of Life and the Eucharist with the Last Supper when the Mass was instituted. Liturgically, the emphasis on Maundy Thursday had been laid on the Mandatum, the new commandment to love one another, symbolised by the washing of the feet, an episode, incidentally, found, like so many other liturgically important incidents, only in St John's Gospel, which does not include the Institution of the Eucharist. The Mandatum is, therefore, always an important episode in the Last Supper plays; in two of the French plays it is preceded by the liturgically associated scene of Mary Magdalen anointing Christ's feet with ointment and washing them with her tears (a similar scene is found in the English N. town play). The conjunction of the two episodes is particularly appropriate when we realise that Maundy Thursday was the day for the blessing of the Holy Oils used in the Sacrament of Supreme Unction: 'what she has done she has done for my burial' (John XII, 7) and also the day for the reconciliation of the penitents before Easter. So much had the Mandatum become the dominant theme on Maundy Thursday, that the Feast of Corpus Christi was established in the late thirteenth century to reaffirm the importance of the gift of the Corpus Domini and the Institution of the Mass on that day. The Corpus Christi procession rapidly became part of a major festival in the Church year and in many countries, notably England, Germany and Spain, the celebration was often enhanced by the performance of plays. It has generally been accepted that there is no dramatic association with the feast in France. However, an examination of the Last Supper scenes in certain passion plays reveals some interesting traits.

In the Ste-Geneviève play, the meal takes place in the house of one Simon[20] and includes the presence of Lazarus with his narrative of the pains of Hell. This is usually found earlier in the play, but in this version Lazarus links his tale with the occasion by relating how the devil '. . . fait le prestre/En lieu de pain feu leur fait pestre' (887–8); after the washing of feet, Christ picks up the theme by telling his disciples 'Et sy vous vueil touz ordener/A prestres et vous vueil donner/le Saint Sacrement d l'autel/Et chascun face a Dieu autel,/Comme vous voierrez que feray' (1029–33). The rest of the scene is more or less biblical in language.

Semur also sets the meal in the house of Simon, here identified as Hospes, and adds a stage direction: 'Hic debeant habere hostias pulcras et rotondas et calices et vinum' (5462). The words of Institution are also changed: 'Mon testament faix en tel guise:/Ou sacrement de saincte Eglise/Je laiz mon corps a mes amis' (6024–6). After blessing the hosts and wine, Jesus gives Judas, instead of the customary sop de 'pain brun' (Greban 18207), an intincted wafer: 'Hic intingat panem in vinum' (6042). The scene ends abruptly with Judas's exit.

Greban is more or less biblical in the form of Institution and his variants on the scene are dramatic rather than sacramental, but Christ does begin the Institution with the words: 'A tous vous vouldray departir/Mon corps sacramentelement/Et faire le saint sacrement/Qui a vostre salut vouldra' (18060–3).

Not surprisingly, the most fully developed scene is in Michel, whose play covers only the life of Christ from Baptism to Burial in 30,000 lines. Here we have a complete Last Supper — roast lamb eaten with 'bitter herbs' (Michel prescribes green lettuce 'en des plats turquins' (17973); and Mons, which is following Michel here, also has lettuce); washing of feet; warning of betrayal; the sop to Judas; interlaced with scenes of preparation for the arrest of Christ. Then comes an important new stage direction. 'Icy fault entendre que les apostres osteront tout de desus la table et n'y demourra que la touaille, puis y metront .i. calice au meilleu et des hosties' (18803). Christ takes a host 'et la tient a la main gauche et mect la main dextre dessus' (18860). To the words of the Institution he adds 'le pain vous transsubstancieres en moy eternel et divin' (18864). Then he takes the cup and adds 'Semblablement aussi le vin/que vous prendres, soit rouge ou blanc./Et a vous tous certainement/Je vous donne ceste puissance' (18866–71). Christ then gives the communion to each of the apostles, who return thanks for this great sacrament (in words reminiscent of the German Corpus Christi play from Innsbruck) with adoration and expressions of belief — even Thomas has no doubt about this.

In view of these explicit references to transsubstantiation and the sacrament of the altar, and especially of this sequence of speeches by the apostles (which were not used in the Mons text), are we perhaps justified in claiming that in Michel's *Passion* France does have a Corpus Christi play after all?

French Play Texts Cited in the Article
Arranged alphabetically by the short titles used

Actes des Apôtres: Possibly composed by Simon Greban. Unpublished.
Adam: Le Jeu d'Adam (Ordo representacionis Ade), ed. W. Noomen, CFMA (Paris, 1971).
Arras: Le Mystère de la passion . . . d'Arras, ed. J.-M. Richard (repr. Geneva, 1976).
Auvergne: La passion d'Auvergne, ed. G. Runnalls, TLF (Geneva, 1982).
Greban: Le mystère de la passion d'Arnoul Greban, ed. Omer Jodogne (Brussels, 1965).
Harvard: The Baptism and Temptation of Christ, ed. and trans. John R. Elliott, Jr. & Graham Runnalls (New Haven and London, 1978).
Michel: Jean Michel. Le mystère de la Passion (Angers 1486), ed. O. Jodogne (Gembloux, 1959).

Mons: Le livre de conduite du régisseur et le compte des dépenses pour le mystère de la passion joué à Mons en 1501, ed. Gustave Cohen (Paris, 1925).

Ste-Geneviève: Le mystère de la passion Nostre Seigneur du manuscrit 1131 de la Bibliothèque Sainte-Geneviève, ed. Graham A. Runnalls, TLF (Geneva and Paris, 1974).

Semur: The Passion de Semur. Text by P.T. Durbin, ed. Lynette Muir, Leeds Medieval Studies, 3 (Leeds, 1981).

Sponsus: Le Sponsus, mystère des vierges sages et des vierges folles, ed. Lucien-Paul Thomas (Paris, 1951).

Troyes: Le mystère de la Passion de Troyes, ed. Jean-Claude Bibolet, TLF, 2 vols (Geneva, 1987).

Valenciennes 20: La passion de Jesu-Crist en rime franchoise. Bibl. de Valenciennes, no. 421. Unpublished.

Valenciennes 25: La Passion de Jhesu Christ jouee a Val128ciennes l'an 1547. MS Paris, Bibliothèque Nationale, fr. 12536; MS Rot. I-O-3. Unpublished.

Viel Testament: Le mistere du Viel Testament, ed. Baron James de Rothschild, SATF, 6 vols (Paris, 1878).

Notes

1. Bibliographical details of all the French play texts quoted in the paper are given, with their short reference titles, in the list on p. 121. Unless otherwise stated, quotations are by line number; unnumbered stage directions are cited by the last line of the preceding speech.

2. Titles and texts of the Latin plays can be found in the two volumes of Karl Young, *The Drama of the Medieval Church* (Oxford, 1933).

3. See Lynette R. Muir, *Liturgy and Drama in the Anglo-Norman Adam*, Medium Aevum Monographs (Oxford, 1973), p. 80.

4. 'Isidore of Seville (d. 636) mentions, besides the blessing and veiling, the uniting of the bridal pair by the deacon with a white and red ribbon . . .' (L. Eisenhofer and J. Lechner, *The Liturgy of the Roman Rite* (London, 1961), p. 405.). It is most tempting to see an echo of this in the red and white clothes of Adam and Eve and the deacon's vestment worn by the Salvator.

5. Unless otherwise mentioned, all biblical quotations are from the Douai translation of the Vulgate.

6. *Egerer Fronleichnamspiel*, ed. G. Milchsack, Bibliothek des Literarischen Vereins in Stuttgart, 156 (Tübingen, 1881), pp. 13–18.

7. See R. Woolf, *The English mystery plays* (London, 1972), pp. 195–6, for details of the English cycles' treatment of the Purification.

8. Greban and his followers have a similar scene for Herod, but the information about the child is only hearsay, not eyewitness (7189–7200).

9. Mary F. Foley, 'Two versions of the Flood: the Valenciennes twenty-day play and the Mystère de la Passion of Mons', *Tréteaux*, 2, 1 (Maine, 1979), 21–38.

10. See Maurice Accarie. *Etude sur le sens moral de la Passion de Jean Michel* (Geneva, 1979) for a detailed analysis of these biographical elaborations.

11. Jean Bouchet, *Epistres* (facsimile reprint, Mouton, 1969), p. xcii.

12. A number of other 'meanings' in the miracle at Cana are discussed by D.A. Trotter, in 'The influence of Bible commentaries on Old French Bible translations.' *Medium Aevum*, 56 (1987), 257–75.

13. A similar reference is to be found in the English N. town play: 'For o dyscypil is lyche thi mayster in al parayl' (Conspiracy, 636). I am grateful to my colleague Peter Meredith for this reference and for allowing me to quote from his forthcoming edition: *The Passion Play from the N. town Manuscript*, ed. Peter Meredith (London, 1989).

14. M. Blakemore Evans, *The Passion Play of Lucerne* (New York, 1943) (repr., 1975), pp. 200, 202.

15. *Records of Early English Drama: York*, ed. A.F. Johnston and M. Rogerson (Manchester and Toronto, 1979), p. 58 (Last Judgement Play); pp. 285, 309, 358 (Bakers Play of the Last Supper). *REED Chester* ed. Lawrence M. Clopper (Manchester and Toronto, 1979), pp. 78, 91 (Purification.

16. *Il quaderno di segreti d'un regista provenzale del medioevo. Note per la messa in scena d'una Passione*, ed. A. Vitale Brovarone, *Pluteus*, 1 (Alessandria, 1984), 50–3.

17. It is also included in the English N. town play: an angel appears and 'bryngyth to hym a chalys with an host therin' (Betrayal, 936sd). For edition see above, Note 13.

18. There is not room in the present paper to discuss the widely used Trial or Debate in Heaven as a form for presenting God on the stage. See L.R. Muir. 'The Fall of Man in the drama of medieval Europe', *Studies in Medieval Culture X* (Western Michigan University, 1977), pp. 126–9.
19. Guillaume de Deguilleville, *Le pèlerinage de l'ame*, ed. J-J. Sturzinger (Roxburghe Club, London, 1895).
20. There is some confusion even in the Gospels between Simon the Pharisee and Simon the Leper, both of whom entertain Jesus to a meal. In the plays the two are often interchanged or called merely, as here, Simon, (though the host of the Last Supper is not named in the Gospels). Michel's *Passion* conflates Simon the Pharisee with Simon the Leper and then also calls him Simon of Bethany, at whose house Martha helps with the serving (Michel 11745–6; 14848.).

Index